Frank Champion

Campaign hand book and citizen's manual

A brief review of the colonial and constitutional governments of the United States

Frank Champion

Campaign hand book and citizen's manual
A brief review of the colonial and constitutional governments of the United States

ISBN/EAN: 9783337153465

Printed in Europe, USA, Canada, Australia, Japan

Cover: Foto ©ninafisch / pixelio.de

More available books at **www.hansebooks.com**

CAMPAIGN HAND BOOK

AND

CITIZEN'S MANUAL.

A BRIEF REVIEW OF THE

Colonial and Constitutional Governments

OF THE

UNITED STATES,

FROM 1765 TO 1872.

WITH

BIOGRAPHICAL SKETCHES OF THE PRESIDENTS,

AND

PRESIDENTIAL CANDIDATES.

TOGETHER WITH

DECLARATIONS, CONSTITUTIONS, CONVENTIONS, PLATFORMS, ELECTION RETURNS, ANNUAL EXPENDITURES AND INDEBTEDNESS, AND OTHER NUMEROUS STATISTICS.

BY FRANK CHAMPION,
(Counselor at Law.)

HARTFORD, CONN.:
F. C. BLISS & COMPANY.
1872.

INTRODUCTION.

In the compilation of this little work, the Author has collected together the most important facts, and statistics, relating to the Political History of the country.

In its arrangement he has adopted the simplest form; that of placing events as much as possible in their chronological order, commencing with the Colonial Government, and bringing it down to the present time; introducing the Constitution, Declaration of Independence, Articles of Confederation, &c., in their appropriate places.

In preparing the Biographical Sketches of the Presidents, and of the Candidates recently nominated for the Presidency and Vice-Presidency, he has endeavored to do equal justice to all, giving the facts, without favor or prejudice, and not at all biassed by party views or interest. The Statistical matter has been obtained from reliable and official sources, and great pains has been taken to make it correct in every particular.

In presenting the work to the public, the Author trusts it will be found very useful as a book of reference to all, and especially to those, who may not have access, at all times, to large libraries, where the facts herein stated might be obtained, though not without much trouble.

It is essential to the very existence and duration of our Political Institutions, that the people take a lively interest in our public concerns. They should become thoroughly instructed in the Political History of the country; the Principles of the Government, the Character and Qualifications of the Candidates; and in this connection, we must not forget that a rumor does not prove a fact, a simple fact does not prove a theory, nor a mere *caricature*, in an illlustrated newspaper, prove a man to be either a simpleton, or a knave.

In a free government, like ours, there will naturally arise, at least two great and leading divisions. Men differently educated, and looking at questions from different standpoints, even retaining their integrity, will widely but honestly differ in their opinions on questions constantly arising; hence there ever will be Cliques, Parties, and Factions.

No Party or Faction should receive the continued confidence and support of an American Citizen, unless first, its principles are sound and correct, and second, unless it presents as its candidates to represent those principles, and to occupy its places of trust and emolument, honest, trust-worthy, and capable men.

HARTFORD, July, 1872.

CONTENTS.

	Page.
OUR REPUBLIC	15
ITS PRESENT AREA, AND HOW ACQUIRED	15
ITS POPULATION AT EACH CENSUS PERIOD	16
TABLE OF POPULATION OF STATES AT DIFFERENT PERIODS	17
OUR REPUBLICAN GOVERNMENT	18
THE COLONIAL OR REVOLUTIONARY GOVERNMENT	19
DECLARATION OF INDEPENDENCE	21
COLONIAL GOVERNMENT UNDER THE CONFEDERATION	27
ARTICLES OF CONFEDERATION	28
SERIOUS DEFECTS IN THIS FORM OF GOVERNMENT	39
TABLE, SHOWING THE INEQUALITY OF REPRESENTATION	40
THE FOREIGN DEBT BEFORE THE CONSTITUTION	41
WHY, AND HOW THE CONSTITUTION WAS ADOPTED	42
GENERAL INDEX TO THE CONSTITUTION	43
CONSTITUTION OF THE UNITED STATES	45
AMENDMENTS TO THE CONSTITUTION	60
THE GOVERNMENT UNDER THE CONSTITUTION	73
WHEN RATIFIED BY THE ORIGINAL STATES	73
THE EXECUTIVE BRANCH OF THE GOVERNMENT	75
THE PRESIDENT AND VICE-PRESIDENT, HOW ELECTED	75
PRESIDENTIAL ELECTORS, HOW APPOINTED	77
TABLE OF APPORTIONMENT OF REPRESENTATIVES	78
ELECTORAL VOTE FOR NEXT PRESIDENTIAL ELECTION	78
THE CABINET COUNCIL	79
SECRETARIES OF DIFFERENT DEPARTMENTS	79
THEIR OFFICIAL DUTIES	80
THE LEGISLATIVE BRANCH OF THE GOVERNMENT	81
SENATE AND HOUSE OF REPRESENTATIVES	81
QUALIFICATIONS OF SENATORS AND REPRESENTATIVES	81
THE JUDICIAL DEPARTMENT OF THE GOVERNMENT	82
THE FEDERAL COURTS OF THE UNITED STATES	82
JUDGES OF FEDERAL COURTS, HOW APPOINTED	83

CONTENTS.

Table, showing Salaries of Federal Officers	84
Presidents of the Continental Congress	84
Signers of the Declaration of Independence	85
Table, giving Time of their Births and Deaths	85
Presidents of the United States	86
Vice-Presidents of the United States	86
Secretaries of State, and of the Treasury	87
Secretaries of Other Departments	88
Chief Justices of the U. S. Supreme Court	89
Associate Justices of the U. S. Supreme Court	89
Speakers of the House of Representatives	90
Existing Government of the United States	93
Names of Different Officials	93
Present Senators, Duration of Term, &c	95
Present Representatives, Duration of Term, &c	97
Governments of the Several States	101
Governors of the Several States, and their Salaries, &c	101
When Legislatures Meet—Sessions—State Elections	102
Results at the Latest State Elections	103
Majorities on Joint Ballot, in the Several Legislatures	107
Washington's Administration, Cabinet, &c	109
Financial Condition of the Country	109
Table of Annual Imports, Exports, Expenditures and Debt	109
Biographical Sketch of George Washington	110
Administration of John Adams, and Cabinet	114
Table of Annual Imports, Exports, Expenditures and Debt	114
Biographical Sketch of John Adams	115
Jefferson's Administration, Cabinet, &c	118
Table of Annual Exports, Imports, Expenditures and Debt	118
Biographical Sketch of Thomas Jefferson	119
Madison's Administration, Cabinet, &c	122
Table showing the Financial Condition of the Country	122
Biographical Sketch of James Madison	123
Monroe's Administration, Cabinet, &c	126
Table showing the Financial Condition of the Country	126
Biographical Sketch of James Monroe	127
Administration of John Quincy Adams, Cabinet, &c	130
Table of Finances, Debt, &c	130

CONTENTS.

BIOGRAPHICAL SKETCH OF JOHN Q. ADAMS.........................	131
JACKSON'S ADMINISTRATION, CABINET, &C	134
TABLE OF ANNUAL EXPENDITURES, DEBT, &C	134
BIOGRAPHICAL SKETCH OF ANDREW JACKSON	135
VAN BUREN'S AMINISTRATION, CABINET, &C	140
TABLE OF EXPENDITURES, DEBT, &C	140
BIOGRAPHICAL SKETCH OF MARTIN VAN BUREN.....................	141
HARRISON'S AND TYLER'S ADMINISTRATIONS, CABINETS, &C	144
TABLE OF ANNUAL EXPENDITURES, DEBT, &C	144
BIOGRAPHICAL SKETCH OF WILLIAM H. HARRISON...................	145
BIOGRAPHICAL SKETCH OF JOHN TYLER,..............................	147
ADMINISTRATION OF JAMES K. POLK, CABINET, &C................	150
TABLE OF ANNUAL EXPENDITURES, DEBT, &C	150
BIOGRAPHICAL SKETCH OF JAMES K. POLK	151
TAYLOR'S AND FILLMORE'S ADMINISTRATIONS........................	154
TABLE OF ANNUAL EXPENDITURES, DEBT, &C	154
BIOGRAPHICAL SKETCH OF ZACHARY TAYLOR	155
BIOGRAPHICAL SKETCH OF MILLARD FILLMORE......................	157
ADMINISTRATION OF FRANKLIN PIERCE, CABINET, &C..............	160
TABLE, SHOWING FINANCIAL CONDITION OF COUNTRY.............	160
BIOGRAPHICAL SKETCH OF FRANKLIN PIERCE........................	161
BUCHANAN'S ADMINISTRATION, CABINET, &C......	164
TABLE OF ANNUAL EXPENDITURES, DEBT, &C	164
BIOGRAPHICAL SKETCH OF JAMES BUCHANAN	165
LINCOLN'S ADMINISTRATION, CABINET, &C	168
TABLE OF EXPENDITURES, DEBT, &C	168
BIOGRAPHICAL SKETCH OF ABRAHAM LINCOLN	169
JOHNSON'S ADMINISTRATION, CABINET, &C...........................	173
TABLE OF ANNUAL EXPENDITURES, DEBT, &C	173
BIOGRAPHICAL SKETCH OF ANDREW JOHNSON......................	174
GRANT'S ADMINISTRATION, CABINET, &C.............................	177
FINANCIAL CONDITION OF THE COUNTRY.............................	177
BIOGRAPHICAL SKETCH OF ULYSSES S. GRANT........	178
ELECTORAL VOTE FOR PRESIDENT AND VICE-PRESIDENT,1789–1797..	184
" " " " " " " 1797–1809..	185
" " " " " " " 1809–1817..	186
" " " " " " " 1817–1829..	187
" " " 1829–1841..	188

CONTENTS.

ELECTORAL VOTE FOR PRESIDENT AND VICE-PRESIDENT, 1841–1853	189
" " " " " " " 1853–1865	190
" " " " " " " 1865–1873	191
TABLE OF THE POPULAR AND ELECTORAL VOTE OF 1868 BY STATES	192
LIBERAL REPUBLICAN CONVENTION	194
ADDRESS TO THE LIBERAL REPUBLICAN CONVENTION	195
PLATFORM OF " " " "	196
NOMINATION OF HORACE GREELEY	198
NOMINATION OF B. GRATZ BROWN	199
MR. GREELEY'S LETTER OF ACCEPTANCE	200
BIOGRAPHICAL SKETCH OF HORACE GREELEY	204
BIOGRAPHICAL SKETCH OF B. GRATZ BROWN	208
NATIONAL REPUBLICAN CONVENTION	211
NOMINATION OF ULYSSES S. GRANT	212
PLATFORM OF THE NATIONAL REPUBLICAN CONVENTION	313
NOMINATION OF HENRY WILSON	216
PRESIDENT GRANT'S LETTER OF ACCEPTANCE	217
MR. WILSON'S LETTER OF ACCEPTANCE	218
BIOGRAPHICAL SKETCH OF HENRY WILSON	221
DEMOCRATIC NATIONAL CONVENTION	224
NOMINATION OF GREELEY AND BROWN	226
MEETING OF THE DEMOCRATIC COMMITTEE	227
GREELEY'S FORMAL ACCEPTANCE	229
NATIONAL PROSPERITY	232

ILLUSTRATIONS.

	Page.
THE NATIONAL CAPITOL..FRONTISPIECE	
BILL OF CREDIT OR CONTINENTAL MONEY............................	20
INDEPENDENCE SQUARE—FACE PAGE....................................	21
SEAL OF THE STATE DEPARTMENT..	80
THE NATIONAL SENATE CHAMBER—FACE PAGE......................	81
HALL OF THE HOUSE OF REPRESENTATIVES—FACE PAGE............	100
PORTRAIT OF GEORGE WASHINGTON.....................................	110
" " JOHN ADAMS..	115
" " THOMAS JEFFERSON..	119
" " JAMES MADISON..	123
" " JAMES MONROE...	127
" " JOHN Q. ADAMS..	131
" " ANDREW JACKSON...	135
" " MARTIN VAN BUREN.....................................	141
" " WILLIAM H. HARRISON.................................	145
" " JOHN TYLER..	147
" " JAMES K. POLK..	151
" " ZACHARY TAYLOR..	155
" " MILLARD FILMORE.......................................	157
" " FRANKLIN PIERCE..	161
" " JAMES BUCHANAN..	165
LINCOLN'S INAUGURATION—FACE PAGE................................	263
MEDAL FROM THE FRENCH DEMOCRATS..................................	170
MEDAL TO MRS. LINCOLN...	171
PORTRAIT OF ANDREW JOHNSON...	174
" " ULYSSES S. GRANT..	178
THE WHITE HOUSE FROM PENNSYLVANIA AVENUE—*Face Page*......	192
PORTRAIT OF HORACE GREELEY..	204
" " B. GRATZ BROWN..	208
" " HENRY WILSON...	221

INDEX.

A

Area of the U. S., 15; Its growth, 16; Of the several States, 102.
Articles of Confederation, 28.
Amendments to the Constitution. 60, 71, 74.
Apportionment of Representatives 77, 78.
Attorneys—General, 80, 84, 89.
Arkansas, 17, 101, 102, 107.
Alabama, 17, 101, 102, 107.
Adams, John, Life of, 115—Cabinet, &c.,114. His Administration, 113.
Adams, John Q., Life of, 131—Cabinet &c., 130 — His Administration, 129.
Address of Liberal Republicans, 195
Acceptance, Letters of, 200, 217, 218. Wants in Greeley's last one.

B

Branches of the Government, 75, 81, 82.
Biographical Sketch of Washington, 110.
Biographical Sketch of John Adams, 115.
Biographical Sketch of Jefferson, 119.
Biographical Sketch of Madison, 123.
Biographical Sketch of Monroe, 125.
Biographical Sketch of J. Q. Adams, 131.
Biographical Sketch of Andrew Johnson, 135.
Biographical Sketch of Van Buren, 135.
Biographical Sketch of Harrison, 145.
Biographical Sketch of Tyler, 147.
Biographical Sketch of Polk, 151.
Biographical Sketch of Taylor, 155.
Biographical Sketch of Fillmore, 157.
Biographical Sketch of Pierce, 161.
Biographical Sketch of Buchanan, 165.
Biographical Sketch of Lincoln, 169.
Biographical Sketch of Johnson, 174.
Biographical Sketch of Grant, 178.
Biographical Sketch of Horace Greeley, 204. His Nomination, 198,
Biographical Sketch of Henry Wilson, 220.
Biographical Sketch of B. Gratz Brown, 208. His Nomination, 199,
Buchanan, Life of James, 165. Cabinet, 164.

C

Country—Its Growth and Population, 16, 17. Existing Government, 92.
Colonial Government, 19, 20.
Congress, Continental, 20. Presidents of, 84.

Confederation, Articles of, 28.
Confederate Government—Serious defects in, 39.
Convention of Delegates, to form Constitution, 42
Constitution of the United States, 43. Government under, 73. When Ratified by the States, 73. Amendments to, 45, 60, 71, 74.
Cabinet—Whom composed of, 79.
Cabinet of the Presidents, 109, 114, 118, 122, 126, 130, 134, 140, 144, 150, 154, 160, 164, 168, 173, 177.
Circuit Courts, U. S., 82. Supreme, 82, 93.
California, 17, 101, 102, 107.
Connecticut, 17, 101 102, 107.
Convention, Liberal Republican, 193. Proceedings, &c., 194-199.
Convention, National Republican, 210. Proceedings, &c., 210-216.
Convention, National Democratic, 223. Proceedings, &c., 223-227.
Candidates for the Presidency, &c., 198, 199, 212, 216, 225.

D

Declaration of Independence, 21.
District Courts, U. S., 83.
District Court Judges, 83.
Delaware, 17, 101, 102, 104.
Democratic Convention, Platform and Proceedings, 223-

E

Executive branch of the Government, 75.
Electors, Presidential, 75.
Electors—How Appointed, 76.
Electoral Vote, 78, 184—191.
Existing Government, 93.
Elections, Latest State, 103—107.
Elections—When Held, 102. Presidential, 184—191.

Expenditures of the Government, 109, 114-118, 122, 126, 130, 134, 140, 144, 150, 154, 160, 164, 168. 173, 177.
Exports. See same pages as Expenditures.

F

Florida, 17, 101, 102, 105.

G

Government, Our Republican, 18.
Government, Colonial, 19. Serious Defects in, 39.
Government Under the Constitution, 73. Existing, 93.
Government—Executive Branch, 75 Legislative Branch, 81, Judicial Branch, 82.
Government of the Several States, 101, 102.
Georgia, 17, 101, 102, 105.
Governors of States, 101; When Appointed, Duration of Term, Salaries, &c., 101.
Grant, Ulysses S, Life of, 178; Cabinet, 177; His Renomination, 211; Letter of Acceptance, 217.

H

House of Representatives, 81, 91, 97.
Harrison, Wm. H., Life of, 145; Cabinet, 144.

I

Independence, Declaration of, 21.
Indebtedness of the Country in 1787, 41; at different periods, 109, 114, 118, 122, 126, 130, 134, 140, 144, 150, 154, 160, 164, 168, 173, 177.
Interior, Secretary of, 80, 84, 89.
Illinois, 17, 101, 102, 106.

Indiana, 17, 101, 102, 106.
Iowa, 17, 101, 102, 106.
Impeachment of Andrew Johnson,

J

Justices, U. S. Courts, 83, 84, 89.
Judiciary, 82, 84, 89.
Joint Ballot, Majorities on, 103.
Jefferson, Thomas, Life of, 119; Cabinet, 118.
Jackson, Andrew, Life of, 135; Cabinet, 134.
Johnson, Andrew, Life of, 174; Cabinet, 173; Impeachment, 175.

K

Kansas, 17, 102, 102, 107.
Kentucky, 17, 101, 102, 106.

L

Legislative Branch of Government 81.
Louisiana, 17, 101, 102, 105.
Legislatures—When they Meet, 202.
Lincoln, Abraham, Life of, 169; Cabinet, 168; Death of, 171.
Liberal Republican Convention, 194.
Letters of Acceptance—Greeley's, 200 228; Grant's 217; Wilson's, 218.

M

Ministers, 84, 93, 94.
Ministers, Table of Foreign and Resident, 93.
Maine, 17, 101, 103.
Maryland, 17, 101, 102, 104.
Massachusetts, 17, 101, 102, 103.
Michigan, 17, 101, 102, 106.
Minnesota, 17, 101, 102, 107.
Mississippi, 17, 101 102 105

Missouri, 17, 101, 102, 107.
Madison, James, Life of, 123; Cabinet, &c., 122.
Monroe, James, Life of, 127; Administration, 186.
Medal from French Democrats, to Mrs. Lincoln, 170, 171.

N

National Constitution, 73.
Navy, Secretary of 79; Salary, 84 Table of these Officers, 88.
Nebraska, 17, 101, 102, 107.
Nevada, 17, 101, 102, 107.
New Hampshire, 17, 101, 102, 103.
New Jersey, 17, 101, 102, 104.
New York, 17, 101, 102, 103.
North Carolina, 17, 101, 102, 105.

O

Ohio, 17, 101, 102, 106.
Oregon, 17, 101, 102, 107.

P

Population U S., a Census Period, 16, 17.
Population of the States, 17, 102.
Powers of the Government, 72.
President, 75, 84. Presidential Electors, 75, 76, 77, 78.
Postmaster General, 80, 84, 83.
Presidents Continental Congress, 84; List of, &c., 86; Salary, 84; Electoral Votes for, 184—191.
Pennsylvania, 17, 101, 102, 104.
Polk, James K, Life of, 151; Cabinet, 150.
Pierce, Franklin, Life of 161; Cabinet, 150.
Platforms, of Liberal Republican, 196; of Democratic Party, 224, 196; of Republican Party, 212

R

Republic, Our, 15.
Republican Government, 18
Representative Table, under Confederation, 40.
Representatives, Apportionment of, 78, 82; How Elected, 81; Qualifications, 81; Salaries, 84; Names of present, 97.
Rhode Island, 17, 101, 102, 103.
Returns, State Elections, 103-107. Presidential Elections, 184-191.
Republican Convention, 210; Proceedings, &c., 211.
Republican Liberal Convention, 194, 198.

S

Secretary of State, 79, 84, 87, 93.
Secretaries, Other, 79, 84, 87, 88, 93.
Salaries of Federal Officers, 84.
Senate, 81; Present Members, 95, 96.
Senators, Qualifications of, 81.
Senators—How Classified, 81.
Supreme Court, U. S., 82, 84, 89.
Signers Declaration Independence, 85.
Speakers House Representatives, 90-92.
States, Government of, 101, 102.
State Elections, Results of, 103-107; Time of, 102.
South Carolina, 17, 101, 103, 105.

T

Treasury, Secretary of, 79; Salary, 84.
Table of Secretaries, 87, 88, 89.
Tennessee, 17, 62, 103, 106.
Texas, 17, 101, 102, 105.
Tyler, John, 147; Cabinet, &c., 144.
Taylor, Zachary, Life of, 155; Cabinet, 154.

U

United States, Population, 16, 17.

V

Vice-President—Qualifications and How Elected, 75; His Duties, 75; Salary, 84; Table of Vice-Presidents, 86.
Vermont, 17, 101, 102, 103.
Virginia, 17, 101, 102, 104.
Van Buren, Martin, Life of 141; Cabinet, 140.

W

War, Secretary of, 79; Salary, 84; Table of these Officers, 88.
West Virginia, 17, 101, 102, 104.
Wisconsin, 17, 101, 102, 106.
Washington, George, Biograpical Sketch, 110; His Cabinet and Administration, 190.
Wilson, Henry, Life of, 221. His Nomination, 216. His Letter of Acceptance, 218.

OUR REPUBLIC.

The United States of America, is a Confederation of Sovereign States, and lies in the middle portion of the Western Hemisphere, extending westward to the Pacific Ocean. Its greatest breadth from east to west is about 3,000 miles, and it has a coast line of 2,163 miles on the Atlantic, 1764 miles on the Gulf of Mexico, and 1,343 miles on the Pacific, embracing an area of 3,578,372 square miles.

In 1782, the Territories of the Confederation extended westward to the Mississippi, and northward to the great Lakes, giving a total area of about 800,000 square miles, but by large acquisitions since made, it has reached its present size.

ITS PRESENT AREA HAS BEEN ACQUIRED AS FOLLOWS:

Territory ceded by England in 1783,	815,615	Square miles.
Louisiana, as acquired from France in 1803,	930,928	" "
Florida as acquired from Spain in 1821,	59,268	" "
Texas as admitted to the Union in 1845,	237,504	" "
Oregon by treaty in 1846,	280,125	" "
California taken from Mexico in 1847,	649,762	" "
Arizonia from Mexico by treaty in 1854,	27,500	" "
Alaska from Russia by treaty in 1867,	577,390	" "
Total present Area,	3,578,392	Square miles.

The increase of the population, and the rapid growth and development of the country have been truly wonderful. In 1620 there were but 300 white settlers in New England. Less than 250 years ago, New York City was made up of a dozen log-cabins, and all the land now comprising the City and County of New York, was purchased for the small pittance of twenty-four dollars.

Fifty years since, there were less than 5,000 white people in the vast region between Lake Michigan and the Pacific Ocean, while the population now exceeds 10,000,000. Chicago was then a mere trading-post of half a dozen huts.

Sixty-five years ago, those immense lakes, Ontario, Michigan, Huron, and Superior, were entirely without commerce, and an Indian's canoe was about the only craft seen upon them; but now, they are crowded thoroughfares, and the value of the traffic upon these waters, and navigable rivers, is not much less than nine hundred millions of dollars per annum.

A few years since San Francisco was Mexican territory, with a handful of wild people and almost unknown. She sprang as if by magic into existence, and in the space of two years her population increased from 1,500 to nearly 60,000. Less than a century ago, we were but thirteen feeble Colonies, with but 3,000,000 of inhabitants, while we now comprise 37 free, sovereign, and independent States, having in addition, the District of Columbia and 11 territories, with a population of nearly 40,000,000 of inhabitants.

THE FOLLOWING TABLE WILL SHOW THE POPULATION OF THE COUNTRY, AT THE DIFFERENT CENSUS PERIODS, SINCE, AND INCLUDING 1790.

Census Years.	Whites.	Free Colored.	Slaves.	Total.
1790	3,172,464	59,466	697,897	3,929,827
1800	4,304,489	108,395	8,43,057	5,305,941
1810	5,862,004	186,446	1,191,364	7,239,814
1820	7,866,569	233,524	1,538,098	9,638,191
1830	10,532,060	319,599	2,009,043	12,866,020
1840	14,189,705	386,292	2,487,356	17,069,453
1850	19,630,738	428,661	3,204,089	23,260,484
1860	26,957,471	532,000	3,953,760	31,443,321
1870	33,586,949	4,880,009		*38,555,083

*This total includes 63,254 Chinese and 25,731 Indians.

POPULATION OF THE UNITED STATES,

ACCORDING TO THE CENSUS OF

1840, 1850, 1860 & 1870.

States and Territories.	1840.	1850.	1860.	1870.
Alabama	590,756	771,623	964,201	996,992
Arkansas	97,574	209,897	435,450	484,471
California		92,597	379,994	560,217
Connecticut	309,978	370,792	460,147	537,454
Delaware	78,085	91,532	112,216	125,015
Florida	54,477	87,445	140,424	187,748
Georgia	691,392	906,185	1,057,286	1,184,109
Illinois	476,183	851,470	1,711,951	2,539,891
Indiana	685,866	988,416	1,350,428	1,680,637
Iowa	43,112	192,214	674,913	1,191,792
Kansas			107,206	364,399
Kentucky	779,828	982,405	1,155,684	1,321,011
Louisiana	352,411	517,762	708,002	726,915
Maine	501,793	583,169	628,279	626,915
Maryland	470,019	583,034	687,049	780,894
Massachusetts	737,699	994,514	1,231,066	1,457,351
Michigan	212,267	397,654	749,113	1,184,059
Minnesota		6,077	172,023	439,706
Mississippi	375,651	606,526	791,305	827,922
Missouri	383,702	682,044	1,182,012	1,721,295
Nebraska			28,841	122,993
Nevada			6,857	42,491
New Hampshire	284,574	317,976	326,073	318,300
New Jersey	373,306	489,555	672,035	906,096
New York	2,428,921	3,097,394	3,880,735	4,382,759
North Carolina	753,419	869,039	992,622	1,071,361
Ohio	1,519,467	1,980,329	2,339,511	2,665,260
Oregon		13,294	52,465	90,923
Pennsylvania	1,724,033	2,311,786	2,906,215	3,521,791
Rhode Island	108,830	147,515	174,620	217,353
South Carolina	594,398	668,507	703,708	705,606
Tennessee	829,210	1,002,717	1,109,801	1,258,520
Texas		212,592	604,215	818,579
Vermont	291,918	314,120	315,098	330,551
Virginia	1,239,797	1,421,661	1,596,318	1,225,163
West Virginia				442,014
Wisconsin	30,945	305,391	775,881	1,054,670
Total States	17,019,641	23,067,262	31,183,744	38,113,253
Arizona				9,658
Colorado			34,277	39,864
Dakota			4,837	14,181
District of Columbia	43,712	51,687	75,080	131,700
Idaho				14,999
Montana				20,595
New Mexico		61,547	93,516	91,874
Utah		11,380	40,273	86,786
Washington			11,594	23,955
Wyoming				9,118
Seamen in U. S. Service	6,100			
Totals	17,069,453	23,191,876	31,443,321	38,555,983

OUR REPUBLICAN GOVERNMENT.

The Government of the United States is the result of deep research, cool and calm deliberation, of great wisdom and sound judgment, and is probably the best ever formed by man.

It was not brought about in a hurried manner, nor did it spring into existence, by reason of a combination of unforeseen and fortuituos circumstances, which aroused the passions of the multitude, and led them to adopt a Republican Government more tyrannical than tyranny itself.

Our government was based upon truth and justice, and the object of it was to establish justice, insure domestic tranquillity, provide for the common defence, promote the general welfare, and to secure the blessings of liberty to ourselves and posterity.

The government and constitution being purely Democratic, the People are the Sovereigns. How much is expressed in those three words, "WE, THE PEOPLE;" that is, We, the Sovereigns; We, the Rulers; We, the Law-Givers; how expressive of majesty and power, and how insignificant do they make Kings and tyrants appear. The President, Vice President, Senators, Legislators, and all other officials are the *mere agents* and *servants* of "We, the People," for they were created by, and for the people, and not the people for them. Whatever of power, whatever of authority, whatever of dignity they possess in their official stations, was delegated to them by the Sovereign People for the honor, prosperity, and happiness of the people themselves.

What government, or constitution could be devised, more perfect than that, which puts it in the power of those who suffer from an unprincipled government officer, or from the effects of a mal-administration, to remove such, or prevent their continuance, not by rash, passionate, and unlawful acts as in ancient republics, but by such as are rational, deliberate, and constitutional. This could not be done under a tyrannical, despotic, or monarchial government, because the crown and scepter are hereditary.

THE COLONIAL
OR
REVOLUTIONARY GOVERNMENT.

As early as October 1765, soon after the first encroachment had been made by the British Government upon our liberties, by the passage of the Stamp Act, a congress of delegates from the Colonies of Massachusetts, Rhode Island, Connecticut, New York, New Jersey, Pennsylvania, Delaware, Maryland, and South Carolina, assembled in New York, and adopted a DECLARATION OF RIGHTS, asserting that the sole power of taxation resided in the Colonial legislatures, and that the restrictions imposed upon them by the late acts of Parliament, were unjust and burdensome. An address to the King, and a petition to each house of Parliament were adopted.

Subsequently, on the 4th day of September, 1774, a congress of delegates from all the Colonies excepting Georgia, assembled at Philadelphia, "with authority and direction to meet and consult together for the common welfare." Thus was organized by the people, acting in their sovereign capacity, the first general, or National Government.

The first, and most important of their acts, was a declaration, that in determining questions which should arise in this Congress, *each Colony should have one vote.* They also passed a series of resolutions declaratory of their rights, and appointed a committee to examine into their rights and grievances.

This Continental Congress was continued during the revolutionary war, but finally it was superseded by the government formed under the Articles of Confederation. It was invested by the people with large discretionary powers, such as superintending the affairs of the Union, organizing an army, regulating the land and naval forces, issuing bills of credit known as Continental money, contracting debts, and otherwise assuming all the prerogatives of an Independent Soverignty.

A BILL OF CREDIT, OR CONTINENTAL MONEY.

INDEPENDENCE SQUARE.

DECLARATION OF INDEPENDENCE.

[On Thursday the 4th day of July, 1776, Congress being in session in the great hall of the venerable State House, located in Independence Square, in Philadelphia, Benjamin Harrison of Virginia, reported that the committee appointed for that purpose had agreed to a declaration which they desired him to present, and which, having been read, was agreed to as follows :—]

A DECLARATION

BY THE REPRESENTATIVES OF THE UNITED STATES OF AMERICA, IN CONGRESS ASSEMBLED.

When, in the course of human events, it becomes necessary for one people to dissolve the political bands which have connected them with another, and to assume, among the powers of the earth, the separate and equal station to which the laws of nature and of nature's God entitle them, a decent respect to the opinions of mankind requires that they should declare the causes which impel them to the separation.

We hold these truths to be self-evident, that all men are created equal; that they are endowed by their Creator with certain unalienable rights; that among these are life, liberty, and the pursuit of happiness. That to secure these rights, governments are instituted among men, deriving their just powers from the consent of the governed; that, whenever any form of government becomes destructive of these ends, it is the right of the people to alter or to abolish it, and to institute a new government, laying its foundation on such principles, and organizing its powers in such form, as to them shall seem most likely to effect their safety and happiness. Prudence, indeed, will dictate that governments long established, should not be changed for light and transient causes; and accordingly, all experience hath shown, that mankind are more disposed to suffer, while evils are sufferable, than to right themselves by abolishing the forms to which the are accustomed. But, when a long train of abuses and usurpations, pursuing invariably the same object, evinces a design to reduce them under absolute despotism, it is their right, it is their duty, to throw off such government, and to provide new guards for their future security. Such has been the patient sufferance of these colonies, and such is now the necessity which constrains them to alter their former systems of government. The history of the present King of Great Britain is a history of repeated injuries and usurpations, all having, in direct object, the establishment of an absolute tyranny over these states. To prove this, let facts be submitted to a candid world:

He has refused his assent to laws the most wholesome and necessary for the public good.

He has forbidden his Governors to pass laws of immediate and pressing importance, unless suspended in their operation till his assent should be obtained; and when so suspended, he has utterly neglected to attend to them.

He has refused to pass other laws for the accommodation of large districts of people, unless those people would relinquish the right of representation in the legislature; a right inestimable to them, and formidable to tyrants only.

He has called together legislative bodies at places unusual, uncomfortable, and distant from the depository of their public records, for the sole purpose of fatiguing them into compliance with his measures.

He has dissolved representative houses repeatedly, for opposing, with manly firmness, his invasions on the rights of the people.

He has refused, for a long time after such dissolutions, to cause others to be elected; whereby the legislative powers, incapable of annihilation, have returned to the people at large for their exercise; the state remaining, in the mean time, exposed to all the danger of invasion from without, and convulsions within.

He has endeavored to prevent the population of these states; for that purpose, obstructing the laws for naturalization of foreigners; refusing to pass others to encourage their migration hither, and raising the conditions of new appropriations of lands.

He has obstructed the administration of justice, by refusing his assent to laws for establishing judiciary powers.

He has made judges dependent on his will alone, for the tenure of their offices, and the amount and payment of their salaries.

He has erected a multitude of new offices, and sent hither swarms of officers to harass our people, and eat out their substance.

He has kept among us, in times of peace, standing armies, without the consent of our legislature.

He has affected to render the military independent of, and superior to, the civil power.

He has combined, with others, to subject us to a jurisdiction foreign to our constitution, and unacknowledged by our laws; giving his assent to their acts of pretended legislation;

For quartering large bodies of armed troops among us;

For protecting them, by a mock trial, from punishment, for any murders which they should commit on the inhabitants of these states;

For cutting off our trade with all parts of the world;

For imposing taxes on us without our consent;

For depriving us, in many cases, of the benefits of trial by jury,

For transporting us beyond seas to be tried for pretended offences;

For abolishing the free system of English laws in a neighboring province, establishing therein an arbitrary government and enlarging its boundaries, so as to render it at once an example and fit instrument for introducing the same absolute rule into these colonies;

For taking away our charters, abolishing our most valuable laws, and altering, fundamentally, the powers of our governments;

For suspending our own legislatures, and declaring themselves invested with power to legislate for us in all cases whatsoever.

He has abdicated government here, by declaring us out of his protection, and waging war against us.

He has plundered our seas, ravaged our coasts, burnt our towns, and destroyed the lives of our people.

He is, at this time, transporting large armies of foreign mercenaries to complete the works of death, desolation, and tyranny, already begun, with circumstances of cruelty and perfidy scarcely paralleled in the most barbarous ages, and totally unworthy the head of a civilized nation.

He has constrained our fellow-citizens, taken captive on the high seas, to bear arms against their country, to become the executions of their friends and brethren, or to fall themselves by their hands.

He has excited domestic insurrections amongst us, and has endeavored to bring on the inhabitants of our frontiers, the merciless Indian savages, whose known rule of warfare is an undistinguished destruction, of all ages, sexes, and conditions.

In every stage of these oppressions, we have petitioned for redress, in the most humble terms; our repeated petitions have been answered only by repeated injury. A prince, whose character is thus marked by every act which may define a tyrant, is unfit to be the ruler of a free people.

Nor have we been wanting in attention to our British brethren. We have warned them, from time to time, of attempts made by their legislature to extend an unwarrantable jurisdiction over us. We have reminded them of the circumstances of our emigration and settlement here. We have appealed to their native justice and magnanimity, and we have conjured them, by the ties of our common kindred, to disavow these usurpations, which would inevitably interrupt our connections and correspondence. They, too, have been deaf to the voice of justice and consanguinity. We must, therefore, acquiesce in the necessity, which denounces our separation, and hold them, as we hold the rest of mankind, enemies in war—in peace, friends.

We, therefore, the Representatives of the UNITED STATES OF AMERICA, in GENERAL CONGRESS assembled, appealing to the Supreme Judge of the World for the rectitude of our intentions, do, in the name, and by the authority of the good people of these Colonies, solemnly publish and declare, That these United Colonies are, and of right ought to be, FREE AND INDEPENDENT STATES; that they are absolved from all allegiance to the British crown, and that all political connection between them and the State of Great Britain, is, and ought to be, totally dissolved; and that, as *FREE AND INDEPENDENT STATES*, they have full power to levy war, conclude peace, contract alliances, establish commerce, and to do all other acts and things which INDEPENDENT STATES may of right do. And, for the support of this Declaration, with a firm reliance on the protection of DIVINE PROVIDENCE, we mutually pledge to each other, our lives, our fortunes, and our sacred honor.

The foregoing Declaration was, by order of Congress, engrossed. and signed by the following members:

JOHN HANCOCK.

New Hampshire
JOSIAH BARTLETT,
WILLIAM WHIPPLE,
MATTHEW THORNTON.

Rhode Island
STEPHEN HOPKINS,
WILLIAM ELLERY,

Connecticut.
ROGER SHERMAN,
SAMUEL HUNTINGTON
WILLIAM WILLIAMS,
OLIVER WOLCOTT.

New York.
WILLIAM FLOYD,

PHILIP LIVINGSTON,
FRANCIS LEWIS,
LEWIS MORRIS.

New Jersey.
RICHARD STOCKTON,
JOHN WITHERSPOON,
FRANCIS HOPKINSON,
JOHN HART,
ABRAHAM CLARK.

Pennsylvania.
ROBERT MORRIS,
BENJAMIN RUSH,
BENJAMIN FRANKLIN,
JOHN MORTON,
GEORGE CLYMER,
JAMES SMITH,
GEORGE TAYLOR,
JAMES WILSON,
GEORGE ROSS.

Massachusetts Bay.
SAMUEL ADAMS,
JOHN ADAMS,
ROBERT TREAT PAINE,
ELBRIDGE GERRY.

Delaware.
CÆSAR RODNEY,
GEORGE READ,
THOMAS M'KEAN.

Maryland.
SAMUEL CHASE,
WILLIAM PACA,
THOMAS STONE,
CHARLES CARROLL, of Carrollton.

Virginia.
GEORGE WYTHE,
RICHARD HENRY LEE,
THOMAS JEFFERSON,
BENJAMIN HARRISON,
THOMAS NELSON, JUN.
FRANCIS LIGHTFOOT LEE,
CARTER BRAXTON.

North Carolina.
WILLIAM HOOPER,
JOSEPH HEWES,
JOHN PENN.

South Carolina.
EDWARD RUTLEDGE,
THOMAS HEYWARD, JUN.
THOMAS LYNCH, JUN.
ARTHUR MIDDLETON.

Georgia.
BUTTON GWINNENT,
LYMAN HALL,
GEORGE WALTON.

[The original document containing the autographs of these venerated patriots, is carefully preserved in a glass case in the rooms of the *National Institute* at Washington. Charles Carroll, the last survivor of this noble band, departed this life in 1832 at the age of ninety years.]

COLONIAL GOVERNMENT

UNDER THE ARTICLES OF CONFEDERATION.

In July 1775, previous to the Declaration of Independence, Dr. Franklin submitted to the consideration of Congress, a draft of confederation between the Colonies, but no action thereon seems to have been taken.

On the 11th day of June 1776, it was resolved by Congress, that a committee should be appointed, to prepare the form of a confederation to be entered into between the Colonies, and the next day a committee was appointed, which consisted of one member from each Colony. A report was thereafter made, and the subject from time to time debated, until the 15th of November 1777 when it was finally agreed to.

These Articles however, were to be submitted to the legislatures of the States, and would not become conclusive until ratified by all the States through their delegates in Congress. Maryland for a long time positively refused the ratification, but finally was induced to do so, and her delegates signed the articles on the 1st of March 1781, more than four years after Congress had submitted the same to the States. On the 2d of March Congress assembled under its new powers.

[On the 9th of July, 1778, the Articles were signed by the delegates of New Hampshire, Massachusetts Bay, Rhode Island, Connecticut, New York, Pennsylvania, Virginia, and South Carolina. The ratification of New York was conditional that all the other States should ratify.

The delegates from North Carolina signed the Articles on the 21st of July, 1778; those of Georgia on the 24th of same month; those of New Jersey, November 26th., 1778; those of Delaware, on the 22d. of February and 5th. of May, 1779; and those of Maryland, March 1st., 1781.]

ARTICLES OF CONFEDERATION.

ARTICLES OF CONFEDERATION AND PERPETUAL UNION

Between the States of New Hampshire, Massachusetts Bay, Rhode Island and Providence Plantations, Connecticut, New York, New Jersey, Pennsylvania, Delaware, Maryland, Virginia, North Carolina, South Carolina, and Georgia.

Art. 1. The style of this confederacy shall be, "*The United States of America.*"

Art. 2. Each State retains its sovereignty, freedom, and independence, and every power, jurisdiction, and right, which is not by this confederation expressly delegated to the United States in Congress assembled.

Art. 3. The said States hereby severally enter into a firm league of friendship with each other, for their common defence, the security of their liberties, and their mutual and general welfare, binding themselves to assist each other against all force offered to, or attacks made upon them, or any of them, on account of religion, sovereignty, trade, or any other pretence whatever.

Art. 4. § 1. The better to secure and perpetuate mutual friendship and intercourse among the people of the different states in this union, the free inhabitants of each of these States, —paupers, vagabonds, and fugitives from justice excepted—shall be entitled to all privileges and immunities of free citizens in the several States; and the people of each State shall have free ingress and egress to and from any other State, and shall enjoy therein all the privileges of trade and commerce, subject to the same duties, impositions, and restrictions, as the inhabitants thereof respectively; provided, that such restrictions shall not extend so far as to prevent the removal of property imported into any State, to any other state, of which the owner is an inhabitant; provided also, that no imposition, duties, or restriction, shall be laid by any State on the property of the United States, or either of them.

§ 2. If any person, guilty of, or charged with treason, felony, or other high misdemeanor, in any State, shall flee from justice, and be found in any of the United States, he shall, upon the demand of the Governor or Executive power of the State from which he fled, be delivered up and removed to the State having jurisdiction of his offence.

§ 3. Full faith and credit shall be given, in each of these States, to the records, acts, and judicial proceedings of the courts and magistrates of every other State.

Art. 5. § 1. For the more convenient management of the general interests of the United States, delegates shall be annually appointed in such manner as the legislature of each State shall direct, to meet in Congress on the first Monday in November in every year, with a power reserved to each State to recall its delegates, or any of them, at any time within the year, and to send others in their stead, for the remainder of the year.

§ 2. No State shall be represented in Congress by less than two, nor more than seven members; and no person shall be capable of being a delegate for more than three years, in any term of six years; nor shall any person, being a delegate, be capable of holding any office under the United States, for which he, or any other for his benefit, receives any salary, fees, or emolument, of any kind.

§ 3. Each State shall maintain its own delegates in a meeting of the States, and while they act as members of the committee of these States.

§ 4. In determining questions in the United States in Congress assembled, each State shall have one vote.

§ 5. Freedom of speech and debate in Congress shall not be impeached or questioned in any court or place out of Congress, and the members of Congress shall be protected in their persons from arrests and imprisonments during the time of their going to and from, and attendance on Congress, except for treason, felony, or breach of the peace.

Art. 6. § 1. No State, without the consent of the United

States in Congress assembled, shall send any embassy to, or receive any embassy from, or enter into any conference, agreement, alliance, or treaty with any king, prince, or State, nor shall any person holding any office of profit, or trust under the United States, or any of them, accept of any present, emolument, office, or title, of any kind whatever, from any king, prince, or foreign State; nor shall the United States in Congress assembled, or any of them, grant any title of nobility.

§ 2. No two or more States shall enter into any treaty, confederation, or alliance whatever, between them, without the consent of the United States in Congress assembled, specifying accurately the purposes for which the same is to be entered into, and how long it shall continue.

§ 3. No State shall lay any imposts or duties which may interfere with any stipulations in treaties entered into by the United States, in Congress assembled, with any king, prince, or State, in pursuance of any treaties already proposed by Congress to the courts of France and Spain.

§ 4. No vessels of war shall be kept up in time of peace by any State, except such number only as shall be deemed necessary by the Untied States in Congress assembled, for the defence of such State, or its trade; nor shall any body of forces be kept up by any State, in time of peace, except such number only as, in the judgment of the United States in Congress assembled, shall be deemed requisite to garrison the forts necessary for the defence of such State; but every State shall always keep up a well regulated and diciplined militia, sufficiently armed and accoutered, and shall provide and constantly have ready for use, in public stores, a due number of field-pieces and tents, and a proper quantity of arms, ammunition, and camp equipage.

§ 5. No State shall engage in any war without the consent of the United States in Congress assembled, unless such State be actually Invaded by enemies, or shall have received certain advice of a resolution being formed by some nation of Indians to invade such State, and the danger is so imminent as not to admit of delay till the United States in Congress assembled can be consulted; nor shall any State grant commissions to any ships or vessels of war, nor letters of marque or reprisal, except it be after a declaration of war by the United States in Congress assembled, and then only against the kingdom or State, and the subjects thereof, against which, war has been so declared, and under such regulations as shall be established by the United States in Congress assembled, unless such State be infested by pirates, in which case vessels of war may be fitted out for that occasion, and kept so long as the danger shall continue, or until the United States in Congress assembled shall determine otherwise.

Art. 7. When land forces are raised by any State for the common defence, all officers of or under the rank of colonel, shall be appointed by the legislature of each State respectively by whom such forces shall be raised, or in such manner as such State shall direct, and all vacancies shall be filled up by the State which first made the appointment.

Art. 8. All charges of war, and all other expenses that shall be incurred for the common defence or general welfare, and allowed by the United States in Congress assembled, shall be defrayed out of a common treasury, which shall be supplied by the several States, in proportion to the value of all land within each State, granted to or surveyed for any person, as such land and the buildings and improvements thereon shall be estimated, according to such mode as the United States in Congress assembled shall, from time to time, direct and appoint. The taxes for paying that proportion shall be laid and levied by the authority and direction of the legislatures of the several States within the time agreed upon by the United States in Congress assembled.

Art. 9. § 1. The United States in Congress assembled shall have the sole and exclusive right and power of determining on peace and war, except in the cases mentioned in the sixth Article, of sending and receiving ambassadors; entering into treaties and alliances, provided that no treaty of commerce shall be made, whereby the legislative power of the respective States shall be restrained from imposing such imposts and duties on foreigners, as their own people are subjected to, or from prohibiting the exportation or importation of any species of goods or commodities whatsoever; of establishing rules for deciding in all cases what captures on land or water shall be legal, and in what manner prizes taken by land or naval forces in the service of the United States shall be divided or appropriated; of granting letters of marque and reprisal in times of peace; appointing courts for the trial of piracies and felonies committed on the high seas; and establishing courts for receiving and determining finally appeals in all cases of capture; provided that no member of Congress shall be appointed a judge of any of the said courts.

§ 2. The United States in Congress assembled shall also be the last resort on appeal in all disputes and differences now subsisting, or that may hereafter arise between two or more States concerning boundary, jurisdiction, or any other cause whatever; which authority shall always be exercised in the manner following: Whenever the legislative or executive authority or lawful agent of any State in controversy with another, shall present a petition to Congress, stating the matter in question, and praying for a hearing, notice thereof shall be given by order of Congress to the legislative or executive authority of the other State in controversy, and a day assigned for the appearance of the parties by their lawful agents, who shall then be directed to appoint, by joint consent, commissioners or judges to constitute a court for hearing and determining the matter in question; but if they cannot agree, Congress shall name three persons out of each of the United States, and from the list of such persons each party shall alternately strike out one, the petioners beginning, until the number shall be reduced to thirteen; and from that number not less than seven, nor more than nine names, as Congress shall direct, shall, in the presence of Congress, be drawn out by lot; and the persons whose names shall be so drawn, or any five of them, shall be commissioners or judges, to hear and finally determine the controversy, so always as a major part of the judges, who shall hear the cause, shall agree in the determination: and if either party shall neglect to attend at the day appointed, without showing reasons which Congress shall judge sufficient, or being present, shall refuse to strike, the Congress shall proceed to nominate three persons out of each State, and the secretary of Congress shall strike in behalf of such party absent or refusing; and the judgment and sentence of the court, to be appointed in the manner before prescribed, shall be final and conclusive; and if any of the parties shall refuse to submit to the authority of such court, or to appear or defend their claim or cause, the court shall nevertheless proceed to pronounce sentence, or judgment, which shall in like manner be final and decisive; the judgment or sentence and other proceedings being in either case transmitted to Congress, and lodged among the acts of Congress, for the security of the parties concerned: provided, that every commissioner, before he sits in judgment, shall take an oath, to be administered by one of the judges of the Supreme or Superior court of the State where the cause shall be tried, "well and truly to hear and determine the matter in question, according to the best of his judgment, without favor, affection, or hope of reward." Provided, also, that no State shall be deprived of territory for the benefit of the United States.

§ 3. All controversies concerning the private right of soil claimed under different grants of two or more States, whose jurisdiction, as they may respect such lands, and the States which passed such grants are adjusted, the said grants or either of them being at the same time claimed to have originated antecedent to such settlement of jurisdiction, shall, on the petition of either party to the Congress of the United States, be finally determined, as near as may be, in the same manner as is before prescribed for deciding disputes respecting territorial jurisdiction between different States.

§ 4. The United States in Congress assembled shall also have the sole and exclusive right and power of regulating the alloy and value of coin struck by their own authority, or by that of the respective States; fixing the standard of weights and measures throughout the United States; regulating the trade, and managing all affairs with the Indians, not members of any of the States; provided that the legislative rights of any State, within its own limits, be not infringed or violated; establishing and regulating post offices from one State to another throughout all the United States, and exacting such postage on the papers passing through the same, as may be requisite to defray the expenses of the said office; appointing all officers of the land forces in the service of the United States, excepting regimental officers; appointing all the officers of the naval forces, and commissioning all officers whatever in the service of the United States; making rules for the government and regulation of the said land and naval forces, and directing their operations.

§ 5. The United States in Congress assembled shall have authority to appoint a committee to sit in the recess of Congress, to be denominated, "*A Committee of the States,*" and to consist of one delegate from each State; and to appoint such other committees and civil officers as may be necessary for managing the general affairs of the United States under their direction; to appoint one of their number to preside; provided that no person be allowed to serve in the office of President more than one year in any term of three years; to ascertain the necessary sums of money to be raised for the service of the United States, and to appropriate and apply the same for defraying the public expenses; to borrow money or emit bills on the credit of the United States, transmitting every half-year to the respective States an account of the sums of money so borrowed or emitted; to build and equip a navy;

to agree upon the number of land forces, and to make requisitions from each State for its quota, in proportion to the number of white inhabitants in such State, which requisition shall be binding; and thereupon the legislature of each State shall appoint the regimental officers, raise the men, clothe, arm, and equip them, in a soldier-like manner, at the expense of the United States; and the officers and men so clothed, armed, and equipped, shall march to the place appointed, and within the time agreed on by the United States in Congress assembled; but it the United States in Congress assembled shall, on consideration of circumstances, judge proper that any State should not raise men, or should raise a smaller number than its quota, and that any other State should raise a greater number of men than the quota thereof, such extra number shall be raised, officered, clothed, armed, and equipped in the same manner as the quota of such State, unless the legislature of such State shall judge that such extra number cannot be safely spared out of the same, in which case they shall raise, officer, clothe, arm, and equip, as many of such extra number as they judge can be safely spared, and the officers and men so clothed, armed, and equipped, shall march to the place appointed, and within the time agreed on by the United States in Congress assembled.

§ 6. The United States in Congress assembled shall never engage in a war, nor grant letters of marque and reprisal in time of peace, nor enter into any treaties or alliances, nor coin money, nor regulate the value thereof, nor ascertain the sums and expenses necessary for the defence and welfare of the United States, or any of them, nor emit bills, nor borrow money on the credit of the United States, nor appropriate money, nor agree upon the number of vessels of war to be built or purchased, or the number of land or sea forces to be raised, nor appoint a commander-in-chief of the army or navy, unless nine States assent to the same: nor shall a question on any other point, except for adjourning from day to day, be determined, unless by the votes of a majority of the United States in Congress assembled.

§ 7. The Congress of the United States shall have power to adjourn to any time within the year, and to any place within the United States, so that no period of adjournment be for a longer duration than the space of six months, and shall publish the journal of their proceedings monthly, except such parts thereof relating to treaties, alliances, or military operations, as in their judgment require secrecy; and the yeas and nays of the delegates of each State, on any question, shall be entered on the journal, when it is desired by any delegate; and the delegates of a State, or any of them, at his or their request, shall be furnished with a transcript of the said journal, except such parts as are above excepted, to lay before the legislatures of the several States.

Art. 10. The committee of the States, or any nine of them, shall be authorized to execute, in the recess of Congress, such of the powers of Congress as the United States, in Congress assembled, by the consent of nine States, shall, from time to time, think expedient to vest them with; provided that no power be delegated to the said committee, for the exercise of which, by the Articles of Confederation, the voice of nine States, in the Congress of the United States assembled, is requisite.

Art. 11. Canada acceding to this confederation, and joining in the measures of the United States, shall be admitted into and entitled to all the advantages of this Union: But no other colony shall be admitted into the same, unless such admission be agreed to by nine States.

Art. 12. All bills of credit emitted, moneys borrowed, and debts contracted by or under the authority of Congress, before the assembling of the United States, in pursuance of the present confederation, shall be deemed and considered as a charge against the United States, for payment and satisfaction whereof the said United States and the public faith are hereby solemnly pledged.

Art. 13. Every State shall abide by the determination of the United States in Congress assembled, in all questions which by this confederation are submitted to them. And the Articles of this confederation shall be inviolably observed by every State, and the Union shall be perpetual; nor shall any alteration at any time hereafter be made in any of them; unless such alteration be agreed to in a Congress of the United States, and be afterwards confirmed by the legislature of every State.

And whereas it hath pleased the great Governor of the world, to incline the hearts of the legislatures we respectively represent in Congress to approve of, and to authorize us to ratify the said Articles of Confederation and Perpetual Union, Know ye, that we, the undersigned delegates, by virtue of the power and authority to us given for that purpose, do by these presents, in the name and in behalf of our respective constituents, fully and entirely ratify and confirm each and every of the said Articles of Confederation and Perpetual Union, and all and singular the matters and things therein contained. And we do further solemnly plight and engage the faith of our respective constituents, that they shall abide by the determinations of the United States in Congress assembled, in all questions which by the said confederation are submitted to them; and that the articles thereof shall be inviolably observed by the States we respectively represent, and that the union shall be perpetual. In witness whereof, we have hereunto set our hands in Congress.

Done at Philadelphia, in the State of Pennsylvania, the 9th day of July, in the year of our Lord 1778, and in the third year of the Independence of America.

New Hampshire
JOSIAH BARTLETT,
JOHN WENTWORTH, jun.

Massachusetts Bay
JOHN HANCOCK,
SAMUEL ADAMS,

ELBRIDGE GERRY,
FRANCIS DANA,
JAMES LOVEL,
SAMUEL HOLTEN.
    Rhode Island, &c.
WILLIAM ELLERY,
HENRY MARCHANT,
JOHN COLLINS.
    Connecticut.
ROGER SHERMAN,
SAMUEL HUNTINGTON,
OLIVER WOLCOTT,
TITUS HOSMER,
ANDREW ADAMS.
    New York.
JAMES DUANE,
FRA. LEWIS,
WILLIAM DUER,
GOUV. MORRIS.
    New Jersey.
JNO. WITHERSPOON,
NATH. SCUDDER.
    Pennsylvania.
ROBERT MORRIS,
DANIEL ROBERDEAU,
JONA BAYARD SMITH,
WILLIAM CLINGAN,
JOSEPH REED.

    Delaware.
THOMAS M'KEAN,
JOHN DICKINSON,
NICHOLAS VAN DYKE.
    Maryland.
JOHN HANSON,
DANIEL CARROLL.
    Virginia.
RICHARD HENRY LEE,
JOHN BANISTER,
THOMAS ADAMS,
JNO. HARVIE,
FRANCIS LIGHTFOOT LEE.
    North Carolina.
JOHN PENN,
CONS. HARNETT,
JNO. WILLIAMS.
    South Carolina.
HENRY LAURENS,
WM. HENRY DRAYTON,
JNO. MATTHEWS,
RICHARD HUTSON,
THOS. HEYWARD, jun.
    Georgia.
JNO. WALTON,
EDWARD TELFAIR,
EDWARD LANGWORTHY.

SERIOUS DEFECTS IN THIS FORM OF GOVERNMENT.

This confederation was formed in time of war, and under very unfavorable circumstances in many respects, hence upon trial, it soon became evident that the powers conferred upon the Continental Congress were inadequate to the legitimate objects of an effective national government. More especially was this manifested, when it became necessary to legislate upon matters relating to commerce and taxes.

There was a want of, or *deficiency of coercive power in Congress*. It had not the exclusive power to regulate commerce, to issue paper money, or to enforce the laws made, the rules adopted, or the orders given, and even several of the States began to exercise the sovereign, and absolute right of treating the recommendations of Congress with contempt.

By this political compact, the United States in Congress assembled had rights and powers, *without being able to enforce them.*

Another defect was in the mode of representation, which, before the adoption of the Constitution gave to each State an *equal share of power*, although some were ten times as important as others in population and value of property. The States had each an equal voice and share in the Union. The small State of Delaware for instance, had an equal vote and an equal influence in the National Council with Virginia, although Virginia had to pay for the support of the government, by reason of the number of its inhabitants and value of its property, nearly twelve times as much as Delaware.

The population of Delaware at this time was about 50,000 and its quota of taxes in requisition of Congress was $32,475, while Virginia had a population of 650,000 and its quota of taxes was $371,136. So also Rhode Island had a population of only 59,670, and her quota of taxes was only 46,764, while Massachusetts had a population of about 400,000, and her quota of taxes was $324,746, and yet their representatives and power in Congress were equal.

REPRESENTATIVE TABLE.

IN 1787, UNDER CONFEDERATION.

	Population.	Quota of taxes in requisition of Congress.	Mean proportion of votes.	Number allowed in 1787.
New Hampshire,	150,000	$76,268	3	1
Massachusetts,	400,000	324,746	11	1
Rhode Island,	59,670	46,764	2	1
Connecticut,	192,000	191,133	6	1
New York,	250,000	185,567	7	1
New Jersey,	150,000	120,619	4	1
Pennsylvania,	300,000	296,908	9	1
Delaware,	50,000	32,475	1	1
Maryland,	320,000	204,775	7	1
Virginia,	650,000	371,136	14	1
North Carolina,	300,000	157,732	6	1
South Carolina,	225,000	139,017	5	1
Georgia,	56,000	23,288	1	1

The original articles of confederation were found to be insufficient, and ineffectual in many other important particulars. Public credit could not be supported, collection of taxes could not be enforced, alliances could not be obtained, nor treaties preserved, and what was still more defective, hostilities between the States could not be prevented, nor insurrections among citizens.

In the spring of 1787 the nation seemed to be on the verge of bankruptcy. Congress had previously made a requisition upon the several States, for money to support, and carry on the government but only a few had responded. New York had paid more than her quota, Pennsylvania nearly all of hers, Connecticut and Delaware about one third of their quota, but many had paid comparatively nothing. The interest both on the foreign and domestic debt was rapidly accumulating.

The receipts of money paid into the federal treasury from Nov. 1st, 1781, to Nov. 1st, 1784, a period of three years was only $2,025,089.34 or about $642,000 per annum. For three years previous to 1787, the whole amount in specie paid into the federal treasury, did not exceed $1,400,000, being a little more than $400,000 per annum. The amount paid in, on these requisitions to carry on the government in 1786, was less than $200,000, and this came from two or three States; thus the receipts of the treasury were constantly decreasing, while the expenditures were increasing.

THE FOREIGN DEBT.   41

The foreign debt at this time was $7,000,000 and the interest coming due, and to be paid the early part of 1787, was as follows.

Interest on loans of the King of France,			$240,740
"	"	Spanish loans about	48,000
"	"	Dutch " "	260,000
"	Certificates and foreign officers		22,000

In addition, there would fall due on principal sum and interest, payable during the year 1787, on French and Dutch loans, more than $1,000,000, making in the aggregate $1,600,000 to pay in 1787, and about $1,000,000 annually thereafter, (on an average) for the next ten years on said loans, and then about $300,000 annually, for the next ten years thereafter. In addition to this, there was a large domestic debt, upon which interest was accruing, and the indebtedness increasing.

This was indeed a dark hour for the new Republic. Congress was powerless; she could make requisitions on the several States, but could not compel the payment of a farthing. "The GREAT CRISIS HAD ARRIVED when the people of these United States, by whose will, and for whose benefit, the federal government was instituted had to decide whether they would support their rank as a nation by maintaining the PUBLIC FAITH at home and abroad, or whether for want of a timely exertion in establishing a GENERAL REVENUE, and thereby giving strength to the confederacy, they would hazard not only the existence of the UNION, but of those great and invaluable privileges, for which they have so arduously and so honorably contended."

Previous to this General Washington had addressed his circular letter to the Governors of the several States, urging them in the strongest language to comply with the requisition of Congress, and to preserve the public credit. Many of the States had attempted to do this, but they were impoverished by the continued drain on the people. The war had been long and expensive, the entire cost being estimated at *one hundred and thirty millions of dollars, exclusive of certain losses of forty millions more.*

By reason of this state of affairs in Febuary 1787 a resolution was offered in Congress, that on the second Monday of May following, a convention of delegates, who should be appointed by the several States be held at Philadelphia, for the sole purpose of revising the Articles of Confederation, and reporting to Congress, and the several legislatures, such alterations and provisions therein, as the exigencies of the government required.

In May 1787, the delegates from all the States presented themselves, excepting from New Hampshire and Rhode Island. They were not represented. Washington was chosen president of the convention, and for upwards of four months it continued with closed doors, and it was not till August 6th, 1787, that the committee which had been appointed for that purpose reported a rough draft of the constitution, and finally on the 15th of September 1787, after a warm and lengthy debate, and after many amendments and revisions, a Constitution was adopted.

CONSTITUTION OF THE UNITED STATES.

ARTICLE I.

SECTION 1. Legislative powers; in whom vested.

SEC. 2. House of Representatives, how and by whom chosen—Qualifications of a Representative—Representatives and direct taxes, how apportioned—Census—Vacancies to be filled—Power of choosing officers, and of impeachment.

SEC. 3. Senators, how and by whom chosen—How classified—State Executive to make temporary appointments, in case, etc.—Qualifications of a Senator—President of the Senate, his right to vote—President *pro tem.*, and other officers of Senate, how chosen—Power to try impeachments—When President is tried, Chief Justice to preside—Sentence.

SEC. 4. Times, etc., of holding elections, how prescribed—One Session in each year.

SEC. 5. Membership—Quorum—Adjournments—Rules—Power to punish or expel—Journal—Time of adjournments limited, unless, etc.

SEC. 6. Compensation—Privileges—Disqualification in certain cases.

SEC. 7. House to originate all revenue bills—Veto—Bill may be passed by two-thirds of each house, notwithstanding, etc.—Bill not returned in ten days—Provision as to all orders, etc., except, etc.

SEC. 8. Powers of Congress.

SEC. 9. Provision as to migration or importation of certain persons—*Habeas Corpus*—Bills of attainder, etc.—Taxes, how apportioned—No export duty—No commercial preferences—No money drawn from treasury, unless, etc.—No titular nobility—Officers not to receive presents, unless, etc.

SEC. 10. States prohibited from the exercise of certain powers.

ARTICLE II.

SECTION 1. President; his term of office—Electors of President; number and how appointed—Electors to vote on same day—Qualification of President—on whom his duties devolve in case of his removal, death, etc.—President's compensation—His oath.

SEC. 2. President to be commander-in-chief—He may require opinion of, etc., and may pardon—Treaty-making power—Nomination of certain officers—When President may fill vacancies.

SEC. 3. President shall communicate to Congress—He may convene and adjourn Congress, in case, etc.; shall receive ambassadors, execute laws, and commission officers.

SEC. 4. All civil offices forfeited for certain crimes.

ARTICLE III.

SECTION 1. Judicial power—Tenure—Compensation.

SEC. 2. Judicial power; to what cases it extends—Original Jurisdiction of Supreme Court—Appellate—Trial by jury, except, etc.—Trial, where.

SEC. 3. Treason defined—Proof of—Punishment of.

ARTICLE IV.

SECTION 1. Each State to give credit to the public acts, etc., of every other State.

SEC. 2. Privileges of citizens of each State—Fugitives from justice to be delivered up—Persons held to service having escaped, to be delivered up.

SEC. 3. Admission of new States—Power of Congress over territory and other property.

SEC. 4. Republican form of government guaranteed—Each State to be protected.

ARTICLE V.

Constitution; how amended--Proviso.

ARTICLE VI.

Certain debts, etc., adopted—Supremacy of Constitution, treaties, and laws of the United States—Oath to support Constitution, by whom taken—No religious test.

ARTICLE VII.

What ratification shall establish Constitution.

AMENDMENTS.

I. Religious establishment prohibited — Freedom of speech, of the press, and right to petition.
II. Right to keep and bear arms.
III. No soldier to be quartered in any house, unless, etc.
IV. Right of search and seizure regulated.
V. Provisions concerning prosecution, trial and punishment — Private property not to be taken for public use, without, etc.
VI. Further provision respecting criminal prosecutions.
VII. Right of trial by jury secured.
VIII. Excessive bail or fines and cruel punishments prohibited.
IX. Rule of construction.
X. Same subject.
XI. Same subject.
XII. Manner of choosing President and Vice-President.
XIII. Slavery abolished.
XIV. Citizenship.

WE, the people of the United States, in order to form a more perfect union, establish justice, insure domestic tranquillity, provide for the common defense, promote the general welfare, and secure the blessings of liberty to ourselves and our posterity, do ordain and establish this constitution for the United States of America.

ARTICLE I.

SECTION 1.

1. All legislative powers herein granted shall be vested in a congress of the United States, which shall consist of a senate and house of representatives.

SECTION 2.

1. The house of representatives shall be composed of members chosen every second year by the people of the several states; and the electors in each state shall have the qualifications requisite for electors of the most numerous branch of the state legislature.

2. No person shall be a representative who shall not have attained to the age of twenty-five years, and been seven years a citizen of the United States, and who shall not, when elected, be an inhabitant of that state in which he shall be chosen.

3. Representatives and direct taxes shall be apportioned among the several states which may be included within this Union, according to their respective numbers, which shall be determined by adding to the whole number of free persons, including those bound to service for a term of years, and excluding Indians not taxed, three-fifths of all other persons. The actual enumeration shall be made within three years after the first meeting of the congress of the United States, and within every subsequent term of ten years, in such manner as they shall by law direct. The number of representatives shall not exceed one for every thirty thousand, but each state shall have at least one representative; and until such enumeration shall be made, the state of New Hampshire shall be entitled to choose three; Massachusetts, eight; Rhode Island and Providence Plantations, one; Connecticut, five; New-York, six; New Jersey, four; Pennsylvania, eight; Delaware, one; Maryland, six; Virginia, ten; North Carolina five; South Carolina, five; and Georgia, three.

4. When vacancies happen in the representation from any state, the executive authority thereof shall issue writs of election to fill such vacancies.

5. The house of representatives shall choose their speaker and other officers, and shall have the sole power of impeachment.

Section 3.

1. The senate of the United States shall be composed of two senators from each state, chosen by the legislature thereof, for six years; and each senator shall have one vote.

2. Immediately after they shall be assembled in conse-

quence of the first election, they shall be divided as equally as may be into three classes. The seats of the senators of the first class shall be vacated at the expiration of the second year, of the second class at the expiration of the fourth year, and of the third class at the expiration of the sixth year, so that one-third may be chosen every second year; and if vacancies happen, by resignation or otherwise, during the recess of the legislature of any state, the executive thereof may make temporary appointments until the next meeting of the legislature, which shall then fill such vacancies.

3. No person shall be a senator who shall not have attained the age of thirty years, and been nine years a citizen of the United States, and who shall not, when elected, be an inhabitant of that state for which he shall be chosen.

4. The vice-president of the United States shall be president of the senate, but shall have no vote unless they be equally divided.

5. The senate shall choose their other officers, and also a president *pro tempore* in the absence of the vice-president, or when he shall exercise the office of president of the United States.

6. The senate shall have the sole power to try all impeachments. When sitting for that purpose, they shall be on oath or affirmation. When the president of the United States is tried, the chief justice shall preside; and no person shall be convicted without the concurrence of two-thirds of the members present.

7. Judgment in cases of impeachment shall not extend further than to removal from office, and disqualification to hold and enjoy any office of honor, trust or profit under the United States; but the party convicted shall, nevertheless, be liable and subject to indictment, trial, judgment and punishment, according to law.

Section 4.

1. The times, places and manner of holding elections for senators and representatives shall be prescribed in each state by the legislature thereof; but the congress may at any time by law make or alter such regulations, except as to the place of choosing senators.

2. The congress shall assemble at least once in every year; and such meeting shall be on the first Monday in December, unless they shall by law appoint a different day.

Section 5.

1. Each house shall be the judge of the elections, returns and qualifications of its own members, and a majority of each shall constitute a quorum to do business; but a smaller number may adjourn from day to day, and may be authorized to compel the attendance of absent members, in such manner and under such penalties as each house may provide.

2. Each house may determine the rule of its proceedings, punish its members for disorderly behavior, and with the concurrence of two-thirds, expel a member.

3. Each house shall keep a journal of its proceedings, and from time to time publish the same, excepting such parts as may, in their judgment, require secrecy, and the yeas and nays of the members of either house on any question shall, at the desire of one-fifth of those present, be entered on the journal.

4. Neither house, during the session of congress, shall, without the consent of the other, adjourn for more than three days, nor to any other place than that in which the two houses shall be sitting.

Section 6.

1. The senators and representatives shall receive a compensation for their services, to be ascertained by law, and

paid out of the treasury of the United States. They shall, in all cases except treason, felony and breach of the peace, be privileged from arrest during their attendance at the session of their respective houses, and in going to and returning from the same; and for any speech or debate in either house they shall not be questioned in any other place.

2. No senator or representative shall, during the time for which he was elected, be appointed to any civil office under the authority of the United States, which shall have been created, or the emoluments wherof shall have been increased, during such time; and no person holding any office under the United States shall be a member of either house during his continuance in office.

Section 7.

1. All bills for raising revenue shall originate in the house of representatives; but the senate may propose or concur with amendments as on other bills.

2. Every bill which shall have passed the house of representatives and the senate shall, before it becomes a law, be presented to the president of the United States; if he approve, he shall sign it; but if not, he shall return it, with his objections, to that house in which it shall have originated; who shall enter the objections at large on their journal, and proceed to reconsider it. If, after such reconsideration, two-thirds of that house shall agree to pass the bill, it shall be sent, together with the objections, to the other house, by which it shall likewise be reconsidered; and, if approved by two-thirds of that house, it shall become a law. But in all cases, the votes of both houses shall be determined by yeas and nays, and the names of the persons voting for and against the bill shall be entered on the journal of each house repectively. If any bill shall not be returned by the president within ten days (Sundays excepted) after it shall have been presented to him, the

same shall be a law in like manner as if he had signed it, unless the congress, by their adjournment, prevent its return, in which case it shall not be a law.

3. Every order, resolution or vote, to which the concurrence of the senate and house of representatives may be necessary (except on a question of adjournment), shall be presented to the president of the United States; and, before the same shall take effect, shall be approved by him; or, being disapproved by him, shall be repassed by two-thirds of the senate and house of representatives, according to the rules and limitations prescribed in the case of a bill.

SECTION 8.

The congress shall have power:

1. To lay and collect taxes, duties, imposts, and excises; to pay the debts and provide for the common defense and general welfare of the United States; but all duties, imposts and excises shall be uniform throughout the United States.

2. To borrow money on the credit of the United States.

3. To regulate commerce with foreign nations, and among the several states, and with the Indian tribes.

4. To establish an uniform rule of naturalization, and uniform laws on the subject of bankruptcies throughout the United States.

5. To coin money, regulate the value thereof, and of foreign coin, and fix the standard of weights and measures.

6. To provide for the punishment of counterfeiting the securities and current coin of the United States.

7. To establish post-offices and post-roads.

8. To promote the progress of science and useful arts, by securing for limited times, to authors and inventors, the exclusive right to their respective writings and discoveries.

9. To constitute tribunals inferior to the supreme court; to define and punish piracies and felonies committed on the high seas, and offenses against the law of nations.

10. To declare war, grant letters of marque and reprisal, and make rules concerning captures on land and water.

11. To raise and support armies; but no appropriation of money to that use shall be for a longer term than two years.

12. To provide and maintain a navy.

13. To make rules for the government and regulation of the land and naval forces.

14. To provide for calling forth the militia to execute the laws of the Union, suppress insurrections, and repel invasions.

15. To provide for organizing, arming and disciplining the militia, and for governing such part of them as may be employed in the service of the United States; reserving to the states respectively the appointment of the officers and the authority of training the militia according to the discipline prescribed by congress.

16. To exercise exclusive legislation in all cases whatsoever, over such district (not exceeding ten miles square) as may, by cession of particular states, and the acceptance of congress, become the seat of government of the United States; and to exercise like authority over all places purchased, by the consent of the legislature of the state in which the same shall be, for the erection of forts, magazines, arsenals, dockyards, and other needful buildings; and

17. To make all laws which shall be necessary and proper for carrying into execution the foregoing powers, and all other powers vested by this constitution in the government of the United States, or in any department or officer thereof.

Section 9.

1. The migration or importation of such persons as any of the states now existing shall think proper to admit, shall not be prohibited by the congress prior to the year one thousand eight hundred and eight; but a tax or duty

may be imposed on such importation not exceeding ten dollars for each person.

2. The privilege of the writ of *habeas corpus* shall not be suspended, unless when, in cases of rebellion or invasion, the public safety may require it.

3. No bill of attainder, or *ex post facto* law shall be passed.

4. No capitation or other direct tax shall be laid, unless in proportion to the census or enumeration herein before directed to be taken.

5. No tax or duty shall be laid on any articles exported from any state. No preference shall be given by any regulation of commerce or revenue to the ports of one state over those of another; nor shall vessels bound to or from one state be obliged to enter, clear or pay duties in another.

6. No money shall be drawn from the treasury but in consequence of appropriations made by law; and a regular statement and account of the receipts and expenditures of all public money shall be published from time to time.

7. No title of nobility shall be granted by the United States; and no person holding any office of profit or trust under them shall, without the consent of the congress, accept of any present, emolument, office, or title of any kind whatever, from any king, prince, or foreign state.

Section 10.

1. No state shall enter into any treaty, alliance or confederation; grant letters of marque and reprisal; coin money; emit bills of credit; make any thing but gold and silver coin a tender in payment of debts; pass any bill of attainder, *ex post facto* law, or law impairing the obligation of contracts; or grant any title of nobility.

2. No state shall, without the consent of the congress, lay any imposts or duties on imports or exports, except what may be absolutely necessary for executing its inspection laws, and the net produce of all duties and imposts laid

by any state on imports or exports shall be for the use of the treasury of the United States, and all such laws shall be subject to the revision and control of the congress. No state shall, without the consent of the congress, lay any duty of tonnage, keep troops or ships of war in time of peace, enter into any agreement or compact with another state, or with a foreign power, or engage in war, unless actually invaded, or in such imminent danger as will not admit of delay.

ARTICLE II.

Section 1.

1. The executive power shall be vested in a president of the United States of America. He shall hold his office during the term of four years; and, together with the vice-president chosen for the same term, be elected as follows:

2. Each state shall appoint, in such manner as the legislature thereof may direct, a number of electors equal to the whole number of senators and representatives to which the state may be entitled in the congress; but no senator or representative, or person holding an office of trust or profit under the United States, shall be appointed an elector.

3. The electors shall meet in their respective states, and vote by ballot for two persons, of whom one at least shall not be an inhabitant of the same state with themselves. And they shall make a list of all the persons voted for, and of the number of votes for each; which list they shall sign and certify, and transmit sealed to the seat of government of the United States, directed to the president of the senate. The president of the senate shall, in the presence of the senate and house of representatives, open all the certificates, and the votes shall then be counted. The person having the greatest number of votes shall be the president, if such number be a majority of the whole number of electors appointed; and if there be more than one who

have such majority, and have an equal number of votes, then the house of representatives shall immediately choose, by ballot, one of them for president ; and if no person have a majority, then, from the five highest on the list, the said house shall, in like manner, choose the president. But in choosing the president, the vote shall be taken by states, the representation from each state having one vote; a quorum for this purpose shall consist of a member or members from two-thirds of the states, and a majority of all the states shall be necessary to a choice. In every case, after the choice of the president, the person having the greatest number of votes of the electors shall be the vice-president. But if there should remain two or more who have equal votes, the senate shall choose from them, by ballot, the vice-president.

4. The congress may determine the time of choosing the electors, and the day on which they shall give their votes, which day shall be the same throughout the United States.

5. No person, except a natural born citizen, or a citizen of the United States at the time of the adoption of this constitution, shall be eligible to the office of president; neither shall any person be eligible to that office who shall not have attained to the age of thirty-five years, and been fourteen years a resident within the United States.

6. In case of the removal of the president from office, or of his death, resignation, or inability to discharge the powers and duties of the said office, the same shall devolve on the vice-president ; and the congress may, by law, provide for the case of removal, death, resignation or inability, both of the president and vice-president, declaring what officer shall then act as president; and such officer shall act accordingly, until the disability be removed, or a president shall be elected.

7. The president shall, at stated times, receive for his services a compensation which shall neither be increased nor diminished during the period for which he shall

have been elected; and he shall not receive within that period any other emolument from the United States, or any of them.

8. Before he enter on the execution of his office, he shall take the following oath of affirmation:

"I do solemnly swear (or affirm) that I will faithfully execute the office of president of the United States; and will, to the best of my ability, preserve, protect and defend the constitution of the United States."

Section 2.

1. The president shall be commander-in-chief of the army and navy of the United States, and of the militia of the several states, when called into the actual service of the United States. He may require the opinion, in writing, of the principal officer in each of the executive departments, upon any subject relating to the duties of their respective offices; and he shall have power to grant reprieves and pardons for offenses against the United States, except in cases of impeachment.

2. He shall have power, by and with the advice and consent of the senate, to make treaties, provided two-thirds of the senators present occur; and he shall nominate, and by and with the advice and consent of the senate shall appoint, ambassadors, other public ministers and consuls, judges of the supreme court, and all other officers of the United States whose appointments are not herein otherwise provided for, and which shall be established by law. But the congress may, by law, vest the appointment of such inferior officers as they think proper, in the president alone, in the courts of law, or in the heads of departments.

3. The president shall have power to fill up all vacancies that may happen during the recess of the senate, by granting commissions which shall expire at the end of their next session.

Section 3.

1. He shall, from time to time, give to the congress information of the state of the Union, and recommend to their consideration such measures as he shall judge necessary and expedient. He may, on extraordinary occasions, convene both houses, or either of them; and in case of disagreement between them, with respect to the time of adjournment, he may adjourn them to such time as he shall think proper. He shall receive ambassadors and other public ministers. He shall take care that the laws be faithfully executed; and shall commission all the officers of the United States.

Section 4.

1. The president, vice-president and all civil officers of the United States, shall be removed from office on impeachment for, and conviction of treason, bribery or other high crimes and misdemeanors.

ARTICLE III.
Section 1.

1. The judicial power of the United States shall be vested in one supreme court, and in such inferior courts as the congress may, from time to time, ordain and establish. The judges, both of the supreme and inferior courts, shall hold their offices during good behavior; and shall, at stated times, receive for their services a compensation, which shall not be diminished during their continuance in office.

Section 2.

1. The judicial power shall extend to all cases in law and equity arising under this constitution, the laws of the United States, and treaties made, or which shall be made, under their authority; to all cases affecting ambassadors, other public ministers and consuls; to all cases of admiralty

and maritime jurisdiction; to controversies to which the United States shall be a party; to controversies between two or more states; between a state and citizens of another state; between citizens of different states, between citizens of the same state claiming lands under grants of different states, and between a state, or the citizens thereof, and foreign states, citizens or subjects.

2. In all cases affecting ambassadors, other public ministers and consuls, and those in which a state shall be party, the supreme court shall have original jurisdiction. In all the other cases before mentioned, the supreme court shall have appellate jurisdiction, both as to law and fact, with such exceptions and under such regulations as the congress shall make.

3. The trial of all crimes, except in cases of impeachment, shall be by jury, and such trial shall be held in the state where the said crimes shall have been committed; but when not committed within any state, the trial shall be at such place or places as the congress may by law have directed.

SECTION 3.

1. Treason against the United States shall consist only in levying war against them or in adhering to their enemies, giving them aid and comfort. No person shall be convicted of treason, unless on the testimony of two witnesses to the same overt act, or on confession in open court.

2. The congress shall have power to declare the punishment of treason; but no attainder of treason shall work corruption of blood, or forfeiture, except during the life of the person attainted.

ARTICLE IV.

SECTION 1.

1. Full faith and credit shall be given in each state to the public acts, records and judicial proceedings of every

other state; and the congress may, by general laws, prescribe the manner in which such acts, records and proceedings shall be proved, and the effect thereof.

Section 2.

1. The citizens of each state shall be entitled to all privileges and immunities of citizens in the several states.

2. A person charged in any state with treason, felony or other crime, who shall flee from justice, and be found in another state, shall, on demand of the executive authority of the state from which he fled, be delivered up, to be removed to the state having jurisdiction of the crime.

3. No person held to service or labor in one state under the laws thereof, escaping into another, shall, in consequence of any law or regulation therein, be discharged from such service or labor; but shall be delivered up on claim of the party to whom such service or labor may be due.

Section 3.

1. New states may be admitted by the congress into this Union; but no new state shall be formed or erected within the jurisdiction of any other state, nor any state be formed by the junction of two or more states or parts of states, without the consent of the legislatures of the states concerned, as well as of the congress.

2. The congress shall have power to dispose of, and make all needful rules and regulations respecting, the territory or other property belonging to the United States; and nothing in this constitution shall be so construed as to prejudice any claims of the United States, or of any particular state.

Section 4.

1. The United States shall guarantee to every state in this Union a republican form of government, and shall protect each of them against invasion; and, on application

of the legislature, or of the executive (when the legislature cannot be convened), against domestic violence.

ARTICLE V.

1. The congress, whenever two-thirds of both houses shall deem it necessary, shall propose amendments to this constitution; or, on the application of the legislatures of two-thirds of the several states, shall call a convention for proposing amendments, which, in either case, shall be valid to all intents and purposes, as part of this constitution, when ratified by the legislatures of three-fourths of the several states, or by conventions in three-fourths thereof, as the one or the other mode of ratification may be proposed by the congress; provided that no amendment, which may be made prior to the year one thousand eight hundred and eight, shall in any manner affect the first and fourth clauses in the ninth section of the first article; and that no state, without its consent, shall be deprived of its equal suffrage in the senate.

ARTICLE VI.

1. All debts contracted and engagements entered into before the adoption of this constitution shall be as valid against the United States under this constitution, as under the confederation.

2. This constitution, and the laws of the United States which shall be made in pursuance thereof, and all treaties made, or which shall be made, under the authority of the United States, shall be the supreme law of the land; and the judges in every state shall be bound thereby, any thing in the constitution or laws of any state to the contrary notwithstanding.

3. The senators and representatives before mentioned, and the members of the several state legislatures, and all executive and judicial officers, both of the United States and of the several states, shall be bound by oath or affir-

mation to support this constitution; but no religious test shall ever be required as a qualification to any office or public trust under the United States.

ARTICLE VII.

1. The ratification of the conventions of nine states shall be sufficient for the establishment of this constitution between the states so ratifying the same.

> Done in convention by the unanimous consent of the states present, the seventeenth day of September, in the year of our Lord one thousand seven hundred and eighty-seven, and of the Independence of the United States of America the twelfth. In witness whereof we have hereunto subscribed our names.
>
> GEORGE WASHINGTON,
> *President, and Deputy from Virginia.*

AMENDMENTS TO THE CONSTITUTION OF THE UNITED STATES.

[The following amendments were proposed at the first session of the first congress of the United States, which was begun and held at the city of New York on the 4th of March, 1789, and were adopted by the requisite number of states. Laws of the U. S., vol. 1, page 82.]

[The following preamble and resolution preceded the original proposition of the amendments, and as they have been supposed by a high equity judge (8th Wendell's Reports, p. 100) to have an important bearing on the construction of those amendments, they are here inserted. They will be found in the journals of the first session of he first congress.

CONGRESS OF THE UNITED STATES.

Begun and held at the city of New York, on Wednesday, the 4th day of March, 1789.

The conventions of a number of the states having, at the time of their adopting the constitution, expressed a desire, in order to prevent misconstruction or abuse of its powers, that further declaratory and restrictive clauses should be added, and as extending the ground of public confidence in the government will best insure the beneficent ends of its institution:

Resolved, By the Senate and House of Representatives of the United States of America, in congress assembled, two-thirds of both houses concurring, that the following articles be proposed to the legislatures of the several states, as amendments to the constitution of the United States; all or any of which articles, when ratified by three-fourths of the said legislatures, to be valid to all intents and purposes, as part of the said constitution, namely:]

ARTICLE I.

Congress shall make no law respecting an establishment of religion, or prohibiting the free exercise thereof; or abridging the freedom of speech or of the press; or the right of the people peaceably to assemble, and to petition the government for a redress of grievances.

ARTICLE II.

A well regulated militia being necessary to the security of a free state, the right of the people to keep and bear arms shall not be infringed.

ARTICLE III.

No soldier shall, in time of peace, be quartered in any house without the consent of the owner, nor in time of war but in a manner to be prescribed by law.

ARTICLE IV.

The right of the people to be secure in their persons, houses, paper and effects, against unreasonable searches and seizures, shall not be violated; and no warrants shall issue but upon probable cause, supported by oath or affirmation, and particularly describing the place to be searched, and the persons or things to be seized.

ARTICLE V.

No person shall be held to answer for a capital or otherwise infamous crime, unless on a presentment or indictment of a grand jury, except in cases arising in the land or naval forces, or in the militia, when in actual service in time of war or public danger; nor shall any person be subject for the same offense to be twice put in jeopardy of life or limb; nor shall be compelled, in any criminal case, to be a witness against himself, nor be deprived of life, liberty or property, without due process of law; nor shall private property be taken for public use without just compensation.

ARTICLE VI.

In all criminal prosecutions, the accused shall enjoy the right to a speedy and public trial, by an impartial jury of the state and district wherein the crime shall have been committed, which district shall have been previously ascertained by law; and to be informed of the nature and cause of the accusation; to be confronted with the witnesses against him; to have compulsory process for obtaining witnesses in his favor, and to have the assistance of counsel for his defense.

ARTICLE VII.

In suits at common law, where the value in controversy shall exceed twenty dollars, the right of trial by jury shall be preserved; and no fact tried by a jury shall be otherwise re-examined in any court of the United States, than according to the rules of the common law.

ARTICLE VIII.

Excessive bail shall not be required, nor excessive fines imposed, nor cruel and unusual punishments inflicted.

ARTICLE IX.

The enumeration in the constitution of certain rights shall not be construed to deny or disparage others retained by the people.

ARTICLE X.

The powers not delegated to the United States by the constitution, nor prohibited to it by the states, are reserved to the states respectively, or to the people.

[The following amendment was proposed at the second session of the third congress. It is printed in the Laws of the United States, vol. 1, p. 73, as article 11.]

ARTICLE XI.

The judicial power of the United States shall not be construed to extend to any suit in law or equity, commenced or prosecuted against one of the United States by citizens of another state, or by citizens or subjects of any foreign state.

[The three following sections were proposed as amendments at the first session of the eighth congress. They are printed in the Laws of the United States as article 12.]

ARTICLE XII.

1. The electors shall meet in their respective states, and vote by ballot for president and vice-president, one of whom at least shall not be an inhabitant of the same state with themselves. They shall name in their ballots the person voted for as president, and in distinct ballots the person voted for as vice-president; and they shall make distinct lists of all persons voted for as president, and of all persons voted for as vice-president, and of the number of votes for each; which lists they shall sign and certify, and transmit sealed to the seat of the government of the United States, directed to the president of the senate. The presi-

dent of the senate shall, in the presence of the senate and house of representatives, open all the certificates, and the votes shall then be counted. The person having the greatest number of votes for president shall be the president, if such number be a majority of the whole number of electors appointed; and if no person have such majority, then from the persons having the highest numbers, not exceeding three, on the list of those voted for as president, the house of representatives shall choose immediately, by ballot, the president. But in choosing the president, the votes shall be taken by states, the representation from each state having one vote; a quorum for this purpose shall consist of a member or members from two-thirds of the states, and a majority of all the states shall be necessary to a choice. And if the house of representatives shall not choose a president, whenever the right of choice shall devolve upon them, before the fourth day of March next following, then the vice-president shall act as president, as in the case of the death or other constitutional disability of the president.

2. The person having the greatest number of votes as vice-president shall be the vice-president, if such number be a majority of the whole number of electors appointed, and if no person have a majority, then from the two highest numbers on the list the senate shall choose the vice-president. A quorum for the purpose shall consist of two-thirds of the whole number of senators, and a majority of the whole number shall be necessary to a choice.

3. But no person constitutionally ineligible to the office of president shall be eligible to that of vice-president of the United States.

ARTICLE XIII.

SECTION 1.

Neither slavery nor involuntary servitude, except as a punishment for crime, whereof the party shall have been duly convicted, shall exist within the United States, or any place subject to their jurisdiction.

Section 2.

Congress shall have power to enforce this article by appropriate legislation.

The following is the certificate of the secretary of state of the United States, announcing the ratification of the foregoing article:

WILLIAM H. SEWARD, *Secretary of State of the United States:*

TO ALL TO WHOM THESE PRESENTS MAY COME, GREETING:

KNOW YE, That, whereas the congress of the United States, on the first of February last, passed a resolution, which is in the words following, namely: "A Resolution submitting to the legislatures of the several states a proposition to amend the constitution of the United States.

"*Resolved,* By the senate and house of representatives of the United States of America in congress assembled (two-thirds of both houses concurring), that the following article be proposed to the legislatures of the several states as an amendment to the constitution of the United States, which, when ratified by three-fourths of said legislatures, shall be valid, to all intents and purposes, as a part of the said constitution, namely:"

(See Article XIII, above.)

And whereas it appears from official documents on file in this department, that the amendment to the constitution of the United States proposed as aforesaid, has been ratified by the legislatures of the states of Illinois, Rhode Island, Michigan, Maryland, New York, West Virginia, Maine, Kansas, Massachusetts, Pennsylvania, Virginia, Ohio, Missouri, Nevada, Indiana, Louisiana, Minnesota, Wisconsin, Vermont, Tennessee, Arkansas, Connecticut, New Hampshire, South Carolina, Alabama, North Carolina and Georgia; in all twenty-seven states.

And whereas, the whole number of states in the United States is thirty-six; and whereas, the before specially-named states, whose legislatures have ratified the said proposed amendment, constitute three-fourths of the whole number of states in the United States:

Now, therefore, be it known, that I, WILLIAM H. SEWARD, secretary of state of the United States, by virtue and in pursuance of the second section of the act of congress, approved the twentieth of April, eighteen hundred and eighteen, entitled, "An act to provide for the publication of the laws of the United States, and for other purposes," do hereby certify, that the amendment aforesaid has become valid, to all intents and purposes, as a part of the constitution of the United States.

In testimony whereof, I have hereunto set my hand, and caused the seal of the department of state to be affixed.

Done at the city of Washington, this eighteenth day of December, in the year of our Lord one thousand eight hundred [L. S.] and sixty-five, and of the Independence of the United States of America the ninetieth.

WILLIAM H. SEWARD,
Secretary of State.

ARTICLE XIV.

Section 1.

All persons born or naturalized in the United States, and subject to the jurisdiction thereof, are citizens of the United States and of the state wherein they reside. No state shall make or enforce any law which shall abridge the privileges or immunities of citizens of the United States; nor shall any state deprive any person of life, liberty or property, without due process of law, nor deny to any person within its jurisdiction the equal protection of the laws.

Section 2.

Representatives shall be apportioned among the several states according to their respective numbers, counting the whole number of persons in each state, excluding Indians not taxed. But when the right to vote at any election for the choice of electors for president and vice-president of the United States, representatives in congress, the executive and judicial officers of a state, or the members of the legislature thereof, is denied to any of the male inhabitants of such state, being twenty-one years of age, and citizens of the United States, or in any way abridged, except for participation in rebellion or other crime, the basis of representation therein shall be reduced in the proportion which the number of such male citizens shall bear to the whole number of male citizens twenty-one years of age in such state.

Section 3.

No person shall be a senator or representative in congress, or elector of president and vice-president, or hold any office, civil or military, under the United States, or under any state, who, having previously taken an oath as a member of congress, or as an officer of the United States, or as a member of any state legislature, or as an executive or judicial officer of any state, to support the constitution of the United States, shall have engaged in insurrection or rebellion against the same, or given aid or comfort to the enemies thereof. But congress may, by a vote of two-thirds of each house, remove such disability.

SECTION 4.

The validity of the public debt of the United States authorized by law, including debts incurred for payment of pensions and bounties for services in suppressing insurrection or rebellion, shall not be questioned. But neither the United States nor any state shall assume or pay any debt or obligation incurred in aid of insurrection or rebellion against the United States, or any claim for the loss or emancipation of any slave; but all such debts, obligations, and claims shall be held illegal and void.

SECTION 5.

The congress shall have power to enforce, by appropriate legislation, the provisions of this article.

The following are the certificates of the secretary of state of the United States, announcing the ratification of the foregoing article:

WILLIAM H. SEWARD, *Secretary of State of the United States:*
TO ALL TO WHOM THESE PRESENTS MAY COME, GREETING:
WHEREAS, the congress of the United States, on or about the sixteenth of June, in the year one thousand eight hundred and sixty-six, passed a resolution, which is in the words and figures following, to wit:
"Joint Resolution proposing an Amendment to the Constitution of the United States.
"*Be it Resolved,* by the senate and house of representatives of the United States of America in congress assembled (two-thirds fo both houses concurring), That the following article be proposed to the legislatures of the several states as an amendment to the constitution of the United States, which, when ratified by three-fourths of said legislatures, shall be valid as part of the constitution, namely:"
(See Article XIV, above.)
And whereas, by the second section of the act of congress, approved the twentieth of April, one thousand eight hundred and eighteen, entitled "An act to provide for the publication of the laws of the United States, and for other purposes," it is made the

duty of the secretary of state forthwith to cause any amendment to the constitution of the United States, which has been adopted according to the provisions of the said constitution, to be published in the newspapers authorized to promulgate the laws, with his certificate specifying the states by which the same may have been adopted, and that the same has become valid, to all intents and purposes, as a part of the constitution of the United States;

And whereas, neither the act just quoted from, nor any other law, expressly or by conclusive implication, authorizes the secretary of state to determine and decide doubtful questions as to the authenticity of the organization of state legislatures, or as to the power of any state legislature to recall a previous act or resolution of ratification of any amendment proposed to the constitution;

And whereas, it appears from official documents on file in this department, that the amendment to the constitution of the United States, proposed as aforesaid, has been ratified by the legislatures of the states of Connecticut, New Hampshire, Tennessee, New Jersey, Oregon, Vermont, New York, Ohio, Illinois, West Virginia, Kansas, Maine, Nevada, Missouri, Indiana, Minnesota, Rhode Island, Wisconsin, Pennsylvania, Michigan, Massachusetts, Nebraska, and Iowa;

And whereas, it further appears, from documents on file in this department, that the amendment to the constitution of the United States, proposed as aforesaid, has also been ratified by newly constituted and newly established bodies, avowing themselves to be, and acting as, the legislatures, respectively, of the states of Arkansas, Florida, North Carolina, Louisiana, South Carolina, and Alabama;

And whereas, it further appears, from official documents on file in this department, that the legislatures of two of the states first above enumerated, to wit: Ohio and New Jersey, have since passed resolutions, respectively, withdrawing the consent of each of said states to the aforesaid amendment;

And whereas, it is deemed a matter of doubt and uncertainty whether such resolutions are not irregular, invalid, and, therefore, ineffectual, for withdrawing the consent of the said two states, or of either of them, to the aforesaid amendment;

And whereas, the whole number of states in the United States is thirty-seven, to wit: New Hampshire, Massachusetts, Rhode Island, Connecticut, New York, New Jersey, Pennsylvania, Delaware, Maryland, Virginia, North Carolina, South Carolina, Georgia, Vermont, Kentucky, Tennessee, Ohio, Louisiana, Indiana, Mississippi, Illinois, Alabama, Maine, Missouri, Arkansas, Michigan, Florida, Texas, Iowa, Wisconsin, Minnesota, California, Oregon, Kansas, West Virginia, Nevada and Nebraska;

And whereas, the twenty-three states first hereinbefore named, whose legislatures have ratified the said proposed amendment, and the six states next thereafter named, as having ratified the said proposed amendment by newly constituted and established legislative bodies, together constitute three-fourths of the whole number of states in the United States.

Now, therefore, be it known, that I, WILLIAM R. SEWARD, secretary of state of the United States, by virtue and in pursuance of the second section of the act of congress, approved the twentieth of April, eighteen hundred and eighteen, hereinbefore cited, do hereby certify, that, if the resolutions of the legislatures of Ohio and New Jersey, ratifying the aforesaid amendment, are to be deemed as remaining of full force and effect, notwithstanding the subsequent resolutions of the legislatures of those states, which purport to withdraw the consent of said states from such ratification, then the aforesaid amendment has been ratified in the manner hereinbefore mentioned, and so has become valid, to all intents and purposes, as a part of the constitution of the United States.

In testimony whereof, I have hereunto set my hand, and caused the seal of the department of state to be affixed.

Done at the city of Washington, this twentieth day of July, in the year of our Lord one thousand eight hundred and [L. S.] sixty-eight, and of the Independence of the United States of America the ninety-third.

WILLIAM H. SEWARD,
Secretary of State.

WILLIAM H. SEWARD, *Secretary of State of the United States:*

TO ALL TO WHOM THESE PRESENTS MAY COME, GREETING.

WHEREAS, by an act of congress, passed on the twentieth of April, one thousand eight hundred and eighteen, entitled "An act to provide for the publication of the laws of the United States, and for other purposes," it is declared that, whenever official notice shall have been received at the department of state that any amendment which heretofore has been and hereafter may be proposed to the constitution of the United States has been adopted according to the provisions of the constitution, it shall be the duty of the said secretary of state, forthwith, to cause the said amendment to be published in the newspapers authorized to promulgate the laws, with his certificate, specifying the states by which the same may have been adopted, and that the same has become valid, to all intents and purposes, as a part of the constitution of the United States;

And whereas, the congress of the United States, on or about the sixteenth day of June, one thousand eight hundred and sixty-six, submitted to the legislatures of the several states a proposed amendment to the constitution, in the following words, to wit:

"Joint Resolution proposing an Amendment to the Constitution of the United States.

"*Be it Resolved*, by the senate and house of representatives of the United States of America, in congress assembled (two-thirds of both houses concurring), That the following article be proposed to the legislatures of the several states as an amendment to the constitution of the United States, which, when ratified by three-fourths of said legislatures, shall be valid as part of the constitution, namely:"

(See Article XIV, above.)

And whereas, the senate and house of representatives of the congress of the United States, on the twenty-first day of July, one thousand eight hundred and sixty-eight, adopted and transmitted to the department of state a concurrent resolution, which concurrent resolution is in the words and figures following, to wit:

"IN SENATE OF THE UNITED STATES,
"*July* 21, 1868.

"WHEREAS, the legislatures of the states of Connecticut, Tennessee, New Jersey, Oregon, Vermont, West Virginia, Kansas, Missouri, Indiana, Ohio, Illinois, Minnesota, New York, Wisconsin, Pennsylvania, Rhode Island, Michigan, Nevada, New Hampshire, Massachusetts, Nebraska, Maine, Iowa, Arkansas, Florida,

North Carolina, Alabama, South Carolina and Louisiana, being three-fourths and more of the several states of the Union, have ratified the fourteenth article of amendment to the constitution of the United States, duly proposed by two-thirds of each house of the thirty-ninth congress; therefore,

"*Resolved*, by the senate (the house of representatives concurring), That said fourteenth article is hereby declared to be a part of the constitution of the United States, and it shall be duly promulgated as such by the secretary of state.

"Attest: GEO. C. GORHAM, *Secretary.*"

"IN THE HOUSE OF REPRESENTATIVES,
"*July* 21, 1868.

"*Resolved*, That the house of representatives concur in the foregoing concurrent resolution of the senate, 'declaring the ratification of the fourteenth article of amendment of the constitution of the United States.'

"Attest: EDWD. McPHERSON, *Clerk.*"

And whereas, official notice has been received at the department of state that the legislatures of the several states next hereinafter named, have, at the times respectively herein mentioned, taken the proceedings hereinafter recited, upon or in relation to the ratification of the said proposed amendment, called article fourteenth, namely: The legislature of Connecticut ratified the amendment June 30th, 1866; the legislature of New Hampshire ratified it July 7th, 1866; the legislature of Tennessee ratified it July 19th, 1866; the legislature of New Jersey ratified it September 11th, 1866, and the legislature of the same state passed a resolution in April, 1868, to withdraw its consent to it; the legislature of Oregon ratified it September 19th, 1866; the legislature of Texas rejected it November 1st, 1866; the legislature of Vermont ratified it on or previous to November 9th, 1866; the legislature of Georgia rejected it November 13th, 1866, and the legislature of the same state ratified it July 21st, 1868; the legislature of North Carolina rejected it December 4th, 1866, and the legislature of the same state ratified it July 4th, 1868; the legislature of South Carolina rejected it December 20th, 1866, and the legislature of the same state ratified it July 9th, 1868; the legislature of Virginia rejected it January 9th, 1867; the legislature of Kentucky rejected it January 10th. 1867; the legislature of New York ratified it January 10th, 1867; the legislature of Ohio ratified it January 11th, 1867, and the legislature of the same state passed a resolution in January, 1868, to withdraw its consent to it; the legislature of Illinois ratified it January 15th, 1867; the legislature of West Virginia ratified it January 16th, 1867; the legislature of Kansas ratified it January 18th, 1867; the legislature of Maine ratified it January 19th, 1867; the legislature of Nevada ratified it January 22d, 1867; the legislature of Missouri ratified it on or previous to January 26th, 1867; the legislature of Indiana ratified it January 29th, 1867; the legislature of Minnesota ratified it February 1st, 1867; the legislature of Rhode Island ratified it February 7th, 1867; the legislature of Delaware rejected it February 7th, 1867; the legislature of Wisconsin ratified it February 13th, 1867; the legislature of Pennsylvania ratified it February 13th, 1867; the legislature of Michigan ratified it February 15th, 1867; the legislature of Massachusetts ratified it March 20th, 1867; the legislature of Maryland rejected it March 23d, 1867; the legislature of Nebraska ratified it June 15th, 1867; the legislature of Iowa ratified it April 3d, 1868; the legislature of Arkansas ratified it April 6th, 1868; the legislature of Florida ratified it June 9th, 1868; the legislature of Louisiana ratified it July 9th, 1868; and the legislature of Alabama ratified it July 13th, 1868:

Now, therefore, be it known, that I, WILLIAM H. SEWARD, secretary of state of the United States, in execution of the aforesaid act, and of the aforesaid concurrent resolution of the 21st of July, 1868, and in conformance thereto, do hereby direct the said proposed amendment to the constitution of the United States to be published in the newspapers authorized to promulgate the laws of the United States, and I do hereby certify, that the said proposed amendment has been adopted in the manner hereinbefore mentioned by the st.tes specified in the said concurrent resolution, namely: The states of Connecticut, New Hampshire, Tennessee, New Jersey, Oregon, Vermont, New York, Ohio, Illinois, West Virginia, Kansas, Maine, Nevada, Missouri, Indiana, Minnesota, Rhode Island, Wisconsin, Pennsylvania, Michigan, Massachusetts, Nebraska, Iowa, Arkansas, Florida, North Carolina, Louisiana, South Carolina, Alabama, and also by the legislature of the state of Georgia; the states thus specified being more than three-fourths of the states of the United States.

And I do further certify, that the said amendment has become valid to all intents and purposes, as a part of the constitution of the United States.

In testimony whereof, I have hereunto set my hand, and caused the seal of the department of state to be affixed.

Done at the city of Washington this twenty-eighth day of July, in the year of our Lord one thousand eight hundred and
[L. S.] sixty-eight, and of the Independence of the United States of America the ninety-third.

WILLIAM H. SEWARD,
Secretary of State.

ARTICLE XV.

SECTION 1.

The right of citizens of the United States to vote shall not be denied or abridged by the United States or by any state on account of race, color, or previous condition of servitude.

SECTION 2.

The congress shall have power to enforce this article by appropriate legislation.

The following is the certificate of the secretary of state of the United States, announcing the ratification of the foregoing article:

HAMILTON FISH, *Secretary of State of the United States:*

TO ALL TO WHOM THESE PRESENTS MAY COME, GREETING:

KNOW YE, That the congress of the United States, on or about the twenty-seventh day of February, in the year one thousand eight hundred and sixty-nine, passed a resolution in the words and figures following, to wit:

"A Resolution proposing an Amendment to the Constitution of the United States.

"*Resolved,* By the senate and house of representatives of the United States of America, in congress assembled (two-thirds of both houses concurring), That the following article be proposed to the legislatures of the several states as an amendment to the constitution of the United States, which, when ratified by three-fourths of said legislatures, shall be valid as part of the constitution, namely:"

(See Article XV, above.)

And, further, that it appears from official documents on file in this department, that the amendment to the constitution of the United States, proposed as aforesaid, has been ratified by the legislatures of the states of North Carolina, West Virginia, Massachusetts, Wisconsin, Maine, Louisiana, Michigan, South Carolina, Pennsylvania, Arkansas, Connecticut, Florida, Illinois, Indiana, New York, New Hampshire, Nevada, Vermont, Virginia, Alabama, Missouri, Mississippi, Ohio, Iowa, Kansas, Minnesota, Rhode Island, Nebraska, and Texas; in all, twenty-nine states:

And, further, that the states whose legislatures have so ratified the said proposed amendment constitute three-fourths of the whole number of states in the United States;

And, further, that it appears, from an official document on file in this department, that the legislature of the state of New York has since passed resolutions claiming to withdraw the said ratification of the said amendment which had been made by the legislature of that state, and of which official notice had been filed in this department;

And, further, that it appears, from an official document on file in this department, that the legislature of Georgia has, by resolution, ratified the said proposed amendment:

Now, therefore, be it known, that I, HAMILTON FISH, secretary of state of the United States, by virtue and in pursuance of the second section of the act of congress approved the twentieth day of April, in the year eighteen hundred and eighteen, entitled "An act to provide for the publication of the laws of the United States, and for other purposes," do hereby certify, that the amendment aforesaid has become valid to all intents and purposes as part of the constitution of the United States.

In testimony whereof, I have hereunto set my hand, and caused the seal of the department of state to be affixed.

Done at the city of Washington, this thirtieth day of March, in the year of our Lord one thousand eight hundred and [L. S.] seventy, and of the Independence of the United States the ninety-fourth.

HAMILTON FISH.

THE GOVERNMENT UNDER THE CONSTITUTION.

TIME OF RATIFICATION BY THE ORIGINAL STATES.

After copies of the Constitution had been sent to the State Legislatures, more than a year elapsed, before the requisite number of States had ratified it.

By Convention of Delaware,..............December 7th., 1787.
" " Pennsylvania,.........December 12th., 1787.
" " New Jersey...........December 18th., 1787.
" " Georgia,....................January 2d, 1788.
" " Connecticut,............January 9th., 1788.
" " Massachusetts..........February 6th., 1788
" " Maryland,....................April 28th., 1788.
" " South Carolina,...............May 23d., 1788.
" " New Hampshire,.............June 21st., 1788.
" " Virginia,....................June 26th., 1788.
" " New York, :.................July 26th., 1788.
" " North Carolina,.......November 21st., 1788.
" " Rhode Island,...............May 29th., 1790.

On the 4th of March 1789, the NATIONAL CONSTITUTION went into effect, and became the organic law of the land. The first Congress thereafter, met in the city of New York, and a quorum was formed on the 6th of April, 1789.

The three most important powers of a government are—1st. That of making laws, or the Legislative power. 2nd. That of executing them, or the Executive power. 3rd. That of interpreting the laws, and applying them to individual cases, or the Judicial power. The first is vested in Congress, the second is vested in the President, and the third is vested in one Supreme Court, and such other courts as Congress may establish. The government therefore is divided into three independent branches, to wit—the *Legislative*—the *Executive*, and the *Judiciary*.

After the organization of the new government, the first matters brought before Congress were those pertaining to the financial affairs of the country, and forming a system of revenues, and also the business of organizing the different branches.

There were three departments arranged for the executive, to wit, The *Treasury*, The *War*, and of *Foreign Affairs*, the heads of which were to be styled Secretaries, and were to constitute a Cabinet Council.

A national Judiciary was also established, consisting of a Supreme Court of the United States, having one Chief Justice and five Associate Justices. District Courts were also established, and each State was made a district, and also three Circuit Courts—the States being formed into three circuits. The question as to *amendments* to the Constitution was then brought forward, and also the Bills of Rights proposed by Virginia and New York. Twelve amendments were agreed to by Congress, but only ten of them subsequently ratified by the States.

[These ten amendments were ratified by the constitutional number of States on the 15th of December 1791. Another the *Eleventh* was proposed on the 5th of March 1794, and ratified on the 8th of January 1798. The *Twelfth* was proposed in December 1803, and ratified on the 25th of September 1804. The *Thirteenth* was ratified in 1865, the *Fourteenth* in 1868, and the *Fifteenth* in 1870, all now being a part of the National Constitution.]

THE EXECUTIVE BRANCH OF THE GOVERNMENT.

THE PRESIDENT.

The executive power is vested in a President of the United States of America. He must be a natural born citizen, a resident of the United States for fourteen years, and of the age of thirty-five years or upwards. He holds his office during the the term of four years, and may be re-elected for a second term.

He is the Commander-in-Chief of the army and navy, and with the consent of the Senate, appoints all cabinet, judicial and executive officers; has power to grant pardons and reprieves for offences against the United States, and it is his duty to see that the laws are faithfully executed.

THE VICE-PRESIDENT.

The Vice-President is elected at the same time, in the same manner, and for the same term as the President, and must have the same qualifications. In case of the death or disability of the President, the duties of the office devolve upon the Vice-President during the term. In case of the death or disability of the Vice-President, the president of the Senate, *pro tempore* takes his place.

PRESIDENTIAL ELECTORS.

The present mode of election of the President and Vice-President of the United States, is not, by the the *direct vote of the people*, but through the machinery of an "Electoral College." Each State has as many Electors, as it has Senators and Representatives in Congress, who must be chosen within thirty-four days preceding the first Wednesday of December of the year in which an election of President and Vice-President takes place.

By an Act of Congress, approved January 23rd, 1845, the uniform time for holding elections for Electors in all the States of the Union, was fixed for the Tuesday next after the first Monday, in the month of November of the year in which they are to be appointed. Each State may also by law provide for the filling of any vacancy or vacancies which may occur in its College of Electors, when such College meets to give its electoral vote, and if any State having held an election for the purpose of choosing electors, should fail to make a choice on the day appointed, then the Electors may be appointed on a subsequent day, in such manner as the State shall by law provide

The Electors must meet at the capitol of their respective States, on the first Wednesday of December, and vote by distinct ballots for President and Vice-President, one of whom shall not be an inhabitant of the same State with themselves.

Having made lists of the number of votes cast and for whom given, they must sign, certify, seal up, and transmit them by a special messenger to the President of the Senate, at Washington. These are opened by the President of the Senate, and the votes are counted in the presence of the Senate and House of Representatives, who have convened on a day fixed for that purpose.

The person having the greatest number of votes for President is duly elected, if such a number be a *majority of the whole number of electors appointed.* If no person has such a majority, then from the persons having the highest number, not exceeding three, in the list of those voted for, the House of Representatives shall choose immediately, and by ballot, the President. In case they neglect to do this before the 4th of March following, then the Vice-President shall act as President, as he would in case of the death or other constitutional disability of the President.

PRESIDENTIAL ELECTORS—HOW APPOINTED

After each decennial enumeration, the aggregate representative population of the United States is ascertained by the Secretary of the Interior.

This was *formerly* done by adding to the whole number of free persons in all the States, including those bound to service for a term of years, excluding the Indians not taxed, and three-fifths of all other persons. As the Members os the House of Representatives were limited by Act of May 23d, 1850, to 233, this aggregate representative population was divided by that number, and the quotient, rejecting fractions, if any, was the ratio of apportionment for the several States.

The loss by fractions was made up by assigning to as many States, having the largest fractions, as may be necessary to make the whole number of Representatives 233, one additional Member each, for its fraction. When new States were admitted, Representatives were assigned to such States on the above basis, in addition to the number limited, till the next census. Thus under the census of 1860 the ratio was found to be 126,823.

By a subsequent Act in March 1862, this ratio was changed, and the number of Representatives after March 1863 was increased from 233 to 241, and subsequently increased by addition of new States and an additional Representative to some of the States to 243.

Now add to this 243, (the number of Representatives,) 72, (the number of Senators,) and we have the number of Presidential Electors of 1868, provided the Electoral College had been full, and all the States (37) had been represented; but as Virginia, Mississippi, and Texas had no vote, only 34 States were represented.

APPORTIONMENT OF REPRESENTATIVES.

Prior to 1868 under Census 1860	New Apportionment, Census 1870
Alabama................6	Alabama................8
Arkansas................3	Arkansas................4
California................3	California................4
Connecticut................4	Connecticut................4
Delaware................1	Delaware................1
Florida................1	Florida................2
Georgia................7	Georgia................9
Illinois................14	Illinois................19
Indiana................11	Indiana................13
Iowa................6	Iowa................9
Kansas................1	Kansas................3
Kentucky................9	Kentucky................10
Louisiana................5	Louisiana................6
Maine................5	Maine................5
Maryland................5	Maryland................6
Massachusetts................10	Massachusetts................11
Michigan................6	Michigan................9
Minnesota................2	Minnesota................3
Mississippi................5	Mississippi................6
Missouri................9	Missouri................13
Nebraska................1	Nebraska................1
Nevada................1	Nevada................1
New Hampshire................3	New Hampshire................3
New Jersey................5	New Jersey................7
New York................31	New York................33
North Carolina................7	North Carolina................9
Ohio................19	Ohio................20
Oregon................1	Oregon................1
Pennsylvania................24	Pennsylvania................27
Rhode Island................2	Rhode Island................2
South Carolina................4	South Carolina................6
Tennessee................8	Tennessee................9
Texas................4	Texas................6
Virginia................8	Virginia................9
Vermont................3	Vermont................3
West Virginia................3	West Virginia................3
Wisconsin................6	Wisconsin................8
Total................243	Total................293

ELECTORAL VOTE FOR NEXT PRESIDENTIAL ELECTION.

The total Electoral vote at the coming election for the President is 367; the majority required by the Constitution is therefore 184. The Electors are as follows.

Maine................7	South Carolina................8	Michigan................11
New Hampshire................5	Georgia................11	Florida................4
Vermont................5	Alabama................10	Texas................8
Massachusetts................13	Mississippi................8	Iowa................11
Rhode Island................4	Louisiana................8	Wisconsin................10
Connecticut................6	Ohio................22	California................6
New York................35	Kentucky................12	Minnesota................5
New Jersey................9	Tennessee................11	Oregon................3
Pennsylvania................29	Indiana................15	Kansas................5
Delaware................3	Illinois................21	West Virginia................5
Maryland................8	Missouri................15	Nevada................3
Virginia................11	Arkansas................6	Nebraska................6
North Carolina................11		
Total................367		

THE CABINET.

The Administrative business of the Country is attended to by several officers, having the titles of Secretaries &c. &c., who together form the Cabinet, and they are appointed by the President. It is now composed of the Secretary of State, Secretary of the Treasury, Secretary of War, Secretary of the Navy, Secretary of the Interior, Postmaster-General, and the Attorney-General, who is the legal adviser of the Administration, and the Official law authority. Each of these Secretaries has charge of a separate department.

THE SECRETARY OF STATE

has charge of the *great seal* of the United States, but cannot affix it to any instrument in writing, without authority from the President. He conducts all treaties we make with other powers, attends to the correspondence with our Ministers at foreign courts, and with Ministers of foreign courts residing here; grants passports, &c.

THE SECRETARY OF THE TREASURY

superintends all the financial matters of the Government; the settling of all the public accounts, and recommends to Congress any measure he may deem advisable for the condition of the revenue.

THE SECRETARY OF WAR

has the exclusive control of the military affairs of the Nation, and superintends every department of the same; attends to the making of public surveys; erection of fortifications, &c. The Adjutant-General's office; Quartermaster-General's Bureau; the Ordinance, Typographical, Medical, Engineer, and Subsistence Bureaus, all come under his supervision.

THE SECRETARY OF THE NAVY

superintends generally all naval affairs, and directs the naval forces. The several Bureaus, such as of Docks, of Navy Yards, of Construction, Equipment, and repairs of Ordinance and Hydrography are all under his supervision.

THE SECRETARY OF THE INTERIOR

superintends all matters connected with the public domain, Indian Affairs, Patents, Public Buildings, Pensions, the Census, and the Expenditures of the Federal Judiciary.

THE POSTMASTER-GENERAL

has the charge of all postal arrangements within the United States, as well as with all Foreign States. The Contract Office, the Appointment Office, and the Inspection Office, all come under his supervision.

THE ATTORNEY-GENERAL

is the Law Counsel for the President, and other officers of the Government. He is the Constitutional Adviser of the Government, and defends the same when necessary.

SEAL OF THE STATE DEPARTMEMT.

THE LEGISLATIVE BRANCH OF THE GOVERNMENT.

All Legislative powers are vested in Congress, which consists of a Senate and House of Representatives, analagous to Parliament in Great Britain, which consists of a House of Lords and a House of Commons.

SENATE.

The Senate consists of two members from each State, elected by the Legislature thereof respectively for six years. They are divided into three classes, each one-third, which is renewed biennially. No person can be a Senator, who has not attained the age of *thirty years*, and been nine years a citizen of the United States, and who shall not, when elected, be an inhabitant of the State for which he shall be chosen.

The Vice-President of the United States is *Ex-Officio*, the President of the Senate. Besides its Legislative prerogatives, the Senate is vested with judicial functions, and its members may constitute a High Court of Impeachment; but the sole power of impeachment belongs to the Representatives.

HOUSE OF REPRESENTATIVES.

The members of the House of Representatives are elected by the people, to seats therein for two years, and the number of such members is in accordance with the population of the several States. In order to ascertain the number, each State is entitled to a census, which is taken every ten years, and heretofore in this computation, two-thirds of the Slaves, and Indians not taxed have been excluded. Each State, however, is entitled to one Representative.

To be *qualified* for this office, the person must be at least *twenty-five* years of age, at least seven years a citizen of the United States, and an inhabitant of the State in which he is chosen.

The ratio based on the census of 1790, was one Representative for every 33,500 inhabitants. The ratio according to the census of 1860, was one for every 126,823 persons, the whole number being limited to 233, but subsequently, by Act of March 4th, 1862, and by additional Act of March 3d, 1863, the ratio was changed; the whole number after March 3d 1863 being made 243.

THE JUDICIAL DEPARTMENT OF THE GOVERNMENT.

The Judicial powers of the country are vested in the Supreme, Circuit and District Courts of the United States. These are called the *Federal* Courts. Congress however, may from time to time establish such other and inferior courts, as may be considered advisable.

THE SUPREME COURT OF THE UNITED STATES.

This is the highest Judicial Tribunal in the land. It has a Chief Justice and eight associate Justices. It has *exclusive jurisdiction* in matters between the States, and *appellate jurisdiction* from final decrees and judgments of the Circuit Courts, in cases where the matters in dispute exclusive of costs exceed the sum of $2,000, and from final judgments and decrees of the highest courts of the several States in certain cases. It has also power to issue writs of *prohibition* and *mandamus* in certain cases.

THE CIRCUIT COURTS OF THE UNITED STATES.

They are held by a Justice of the Supreme Court assigned to the Circuit, and by the Judge of the District in which the Court sits, conjointly. They have original jurisdiction concurrent with the courts of the several States, of all suits at Common Law, or in Equity, when the matter in dispute exclusive of costs, *exceeds the sum of five hundred dollars* and the United States are plaintiff, or an alien is a party, or where the suit is between a citizen of the State where the suit is brought and another State.

They have also exclusive cognizance of most of the crimes and offences cognizable under the authority of the United States, and concurrent jurisdiction with the District Court of offences cognizable therein. They have also appellate jurisdiction from judgments and final decrees of the District Courts of the United States, in all cases where the matter in dispute exceeds the sum, or value of fifty dollars.

The trial of *issues of fact* in all suits, excepting those of equity, and admiralty and maritime jurisdiction, is by a jury.

THE DISTRICT COURTS OF THE UNITED STATES.

They have exclusive original jurisdiction of all civil cases of Admiralty and Maritime jurisdiction, including all seizures under the navigation laws, or of impost, or trade of the United States, where they are made upon tide waters, saving however to suitors, the right of a common law remedy where the common law gives it, also of all crimes and offences cognizable under the authority of the United States, committed within their respective Districts, or upon the high seas in certain cases. They have also concurrent jurisdiction with the State Courts in certain cases. The trial is by jury, except in civil cases of Admiralty and Maritime jurisdiction.

JUDGES HOW APPOINTED.

The appointment of all Judges of the Federal Courts is made by the President, by, and with the approval and consent of the Senate, and they hold their offices during good behavior, and can be removed only on impeachment.

SALARIES OF FEDERAL OFFICERS.

President of the United States, per annum,	$25,000.00
Vice President " " " " "	8,000.00
Secretary of State and other Cabinet Ministers, each " "	8,000.00
Chief Justice Supreme Court, " "	8,500.00
Each Associate Justice Supreme Court " "	8,000.00
Senators and Representatives,* " "	5,000.00
Speaker House of Representatives, " "	8,000.00
Secretary of the Senate, " "	3,600.00
Clerk House of Representatives, " "	3,600.00
Superintendent Coast Survey, " "	6,000.00
Ministers Plenipotentiary to Great Britain and France, " "	17,500.00
Ministers Plenipotentiary to Russia, Prussia, Spain, Austria, Italy, China, Brazil and Mexico, " "	12,000.00
Ministers Resident to Portugal and other States, " "	7,500.00
Consul Generals, Per Annum, from $3,000.00 to	6,000.00
Consuls, " " 1,000.00 to	7,000.00
Secretaries of Legation, " " 1,500.00 to	2,700.00

*Senators and Representatives also receive twenty cents per mile as mileage. There is deducted from their salaries $8.00 per diem for each day's absence, unless caused by sickness.

PRESIDENTS OF THE CONTINENTAL CONGRESS.

From 1774 to 1789.

Name.	From what Colony.	When Elected	Born	Died
Peyton Randolph,	Virginia,	Sept 5, 1774	1723	1775
Henry Middleton,	South Carolina,	Oct 22, 1774	....	....
Peyton Randolph,	Virginia,	May 10, 1775	1723	1785
John Hancock,	Massachusetts,	May 24, 1775	1737	1793
Henry Laurens,	South Carolina,	Nov 1, 1777	1724	1792
John Jay,	New York,	Dec 10, 1778	1745	1829
Samuel Huntington,	Connecticut,	Sept 28, 1779	1732	1796
Thomas McKean,	Delaware,	July 10, 1781	1734	1817
John Hanson,	Maryland,	Nov 5, 1781	....	1783
Elias Boudinot,	New Jersey,	Nov 4, 1782	1740	1824
Thomas Mifflin,	Pennsylvania,	Nov 3, 1783	1744	1800
Richard Henry Lee,	Virginia,	Nov 30, 1784	1732	1794
John Hancock,	Massachusetts,	Nov 23, 1785	1737	1775
Nathaniel Gorham,	Massachusetts,	June 6, 1786	1738	1796
Arthur St. Clair,	Pennsylvania,	Feb 2, 1787	....	1818
Cyrus Griffin,	Virginia,	Jan 22, 1788	1748	1810

SIGNERS OF THE DECLARATION OF INDEPENDENCE.

Names	Time and place of birth.			Died.	
Adams, John	Braintree, Mass.	Oct.	19, 1735	July	4, 1826
Adams, Samuel	Boston, Mass.	Sept.	27, 1722	Oct.	2, 1803
Bartlett, Josiah	Amesbury, Mass.	in Nov.,	1729	May	19, 1795
Braxton, Carter	Newington, Va.	Sept.	10, 1736	Oct.	10, 1797
Carroll, Charles	Annapolis, Md.	Sept.	20, 1737	Nov.	14, 1832
Chase, Samuel	Somerset Co., Md.	Apr.	17, 1741	June	19, 1811
Clark, Abraham	Elizabethtown, N. J.	Feb.	15, 1726	Sept.,	1794
Clymer, George	Philadelphia, Pa.	in	1739	Jan.	23, 1813
Ellery, William	Newport, R. I.	Dec.	22, 1727	Feb.	15, 1820
Floyd, William	Suffolk Co., N. Y.	Dec.	17, 1734	Aug.	4, 1821
Franklin, Benjamin	Boston, Mass.	Jan.	17, 1706	April	17, 1790
Gerry, Elbridge	Marblehead, Mass.	July	17, 1744	Nov.	23, 1814
Gwinnett, Button	England.	in	1732	May	27, 1777
Hall, Lyman	Connecticut	in	1731	Feb.,	1790
Hancock, John	Braintree, Mass.	in	1737	Oct.	8, 1793
Harrison, Benjamin	Berkely, Va.			April,	1791
Hart, John	Hopewell, N. J.	about	1715		1780
Heyward, Thomas, Jr.	St. Luke's, S. C.	in	1746	March,	1809
Hewes, Joseph	Kingston, N. J.	in	1730	Nov.	10, 1779
Hooper, William	Boston, Mass.	June	17, 1742	Oct.,	1790
Hopkins, Stephen	Scituate, R. I.	March	7, 1707	July	13, 1785
Hopkinson, Francis	Philadelphia, Penn.	in	1737	May	9, 1790
Huntington, Samuel	Windham, Conn.	July	3, 1732	Jan.	5, 1796
Jefferson, Thomas	Shadwell, Va.	April	13, 1743	July	4, 1826
Lee, Francis Lightfoot	Stratford, Va.	Oct.	14, 1734	April,	1797
Lee, Richard Henry	Stratford, Va.	Jan.	20, 1732	June	19, 1794
Lewis, Francis	Landaff, Wales.	in Mar.,	1713	Dec.	30, 1803
Livingston, Philip	Albany, N. Y.	Jan.	15, 1716	June	12, 1778
Lynch, Thomas, Jr.	St. George's, S. C.	Aug.	5, 1749	Lost at sea,	1779
McKean, Thomas	Chester Co., Pa.	Mar.	19, 1734	June	24, 1817
Middleton, Arthur	Middleton Place, S. C.	in	1743	Jan.	1, 1787
Moris, Lewis	Morrisania, N. Y.	in	1726	Jan.	22, 1798
Morris, Robert	Lancashire, Eng.	Jan.,	1733–4	May	8, 1806
Morton, John	Ridley, Pa.	in	1724	April,	1777
Nelson, Thomas, Jr.	York, Va.	Dec.	26, 1738	Jan.	4, 1789
Paca, William	Wye Hill, Md.	Oct.	31, 1740		1799
Paine, Robert Treat	Boston, Mass.	in	1731	May	11, 1804
Penn, John	Caroline Co., Va.	May	17, 1741	Oct.	26, 1809
Read, George	Cecil Co., Md.	in	1734		1796
Rodney, Cæsar	Dover, Del.	in	1730		1783
Ross, George	New Castle, Del.	in	1730	July,	1779
Rush, Benjamin, M.D.	Byberry, Pa.	Dec.	24, 1745	April	19, 1813
Rutledge, Edward	Charleston, S. C.	in Nov.,	1749	Jan.	23, 1800
Sherman, Roger	Newton, Mass.	April	19, 1721	July	23, 1793
Smith, James	Ireland			July	11, 1806
Stockton, Richard	Princeton, N. J.	Oct.	1, 1730	Feb.	28, 1781
Stone, Thomas	Charles Co., Md.	in	1742	Oct.	5, 1787
Taylor, George	Ireland		1716	Feb.	28, 1787
Thornton, Matthew	Ireland	in	1714	June	24, 1803
Walton, George	Frederick Co., Va.	in	1740	Feb.	2, 1805
Whipple, William	Kittery, Me.	in	1730	Nov.	28, 1785
Williams, William	Lebanon, Conn.	April	8, 1731	Aug.	2, 1811
Wilson, James	Scotland	about	1742	Aug.	28, 1798
Witherspoon, John	Yester, Scotland	Feb.	5, 1733	Nov.	15, 1794
Wolcott, Oliver	Windsor, Conn.	Nov.	26, 1726	Dec.	1, 1797
Wythe, George	Elizabeth City Co., Va.	in	1726	June	8, 1806

PRESIDENTS AND VICE-PRESIDENTS OF UNITED STATES.

PRESIDENTS.

Year of qualific'n.	Name.	Where from.	Term of office.
1789	George Washington	Virginia	8 years.
1797	John Adams	Massachusetts	4 years.
1801	Thomas Jefferson	Virginia	8 years.
1809	James Madison	Virginia	8 years.
1817	James Monroe	Virginia	8 years.
1824	John Quincy Adams	Massachusetts	4 years.
1829	Andrew Jackson	Tennessee	8 years.
1837	Martin Van Buren	New York	4 years.
1841	Wm. Henry Harrison*	Ohio	1 month.
1841	John Tyler	Virginia	3 yrs., 11 mos.
1845	James Knox Polk	Tennessee	4 years.
1849	Zachary Taylor†	Louisiana	1 yr., 4 m., 5 d.
1850	Millard Fillmore	New York	2 yr., 7 m., 26 d.
1853	Franklin Pierce	New Hampshire	4 years.
1857	James Buchanan	Pennsylvania	4 years.
1861	Abraham Lincoln‡	Illinois	4 yr., 1 m., 10 d.
1865	Andrew Johnson	Tennessee.	3 yr., 10 m., 20 d.
1869	Ulysses S. Grant	Illinois	

VICE-PRESIDENTS.

Year of qualification.	Name.	Where from.
1789	John Adams	Massachusetts.
1797	Thomas Jefferson	Virginia.
1801	Aaron Burr	New York.
1804	George Clinton	New York.
1813	Elbridge Gerry	Massachusetts.
1817	Daniel D. Tompkins	New York.
1824	John C. Calhoun	South Carolina.
1833	Martin Van Buren	New York.
1837	Richard M. Johnson	Kentucky.
1841	John Tyler	Virginia.
1842	Samuel L. Southard§	New Jersey.
1845	George M. Dallas	Pennsylvania.
1849	Millard Fillmore	New York.
1851	William R. King§	Alabama.
1853	David R. Atchison§	Missouri.
1855	Jesse D. Bright§	Indiana.
1857	John C. Breckinridge	Kentucky.
1861	Hannibal Hamlin	Maine.
1865	Andrew Johnson	Tennessee.
1865	Lafayette C. Foster§	Connecticut.
1869	Schuyler Colfax	Indiana.

* Died in office April 4, 1841, when Vice-President Tyler succeeded him.
† Died in office July 9, 1850, when Vice-President Fillmore succeeded him.
‡ Assassinated April 14, 1865, when Vice-President Johnson succeeded him.
§ *Ex-officio* as President *pro tem.* of Senate.

SECRETARIES OF STATE.

Names.	State.	Term of Service.	Born	Died
Thomas Jefferson,	Virginia	1789-1794	1743	1826
Edmund Randolph,	Virginia	1794-1795	....	1813
Timothy Pickering,	Massachusetts	1795-1800	1745	1829
John Marshall,	Virginia	1800-1801	1755	1836
James Madison,	Virginia	1801-1809	1751	1837
Robert Smith,	Massachusetts	1809-1811	....	....
James Monroe,	Virginia	1811-1817	1759	1831
John Quincy Adams,	Massachusetts	1817-1825	1767	1848
Henry Clay,	Kentucky	1825-1829	1777	1852
Martin Van Buren,	New York	1829-1831	1782	1862
Edward Livingston,	Louisiana	1831-1833	1764	1836
Louis McLane,	Delaware	1833-1835	1786	1857
John Forsyth,	Georgia	1835-1841	1780	1841
Daniel Webster,	Massachusetts	1841-1843	1782	1852
Hugh S. Legare,	South Carolina	1843-1843	1797	1843
Abel P. Upshur,	Virginia	1843-1844	1790	1844
John C. Calhoun,	South Carolina	1844-1845	1782	1850
James Buchanan,	Pennsylvania	1845-1849	1791	1868
John M. Clayton,	Delaware	1849-1850	1796	1856
Daniel Webster,	Massachusetts	1850-1852	1782	1852
Edward Everett,	Massachusetts	1852-1853	1794	1865
William L. Marcy,	New York	1853-1857	1786	1860
Lewis Cass,	Michigan	1857-1861	1782	....
Jeremiah S. Black,	Pennsylvania	1861-1861	1810	....
William H. Seward,	New York	1861-1869	1801	....
Hamilton Fish,	New York	1869	....	....

SECRETARIES OF THE TREASURY.

Names.	State	When app'd	Names.	State	When app'd
Alexander Hamilton	N. Y	1789	Walter Forward	Penn	1841
Oliver Wolcott	Conn	1795	John C. Spencer	N. Y	1843
Samuel Dexter	Mass	1801	George M. Bibb	Ky	1844
Albert Gallatin	Penn	1802	Robert J. Walker	Miss	1845
George W. Campbell	Tenn	1814	William M. Meredith	Penn	1849
Alexander J. Dallas	Penn	1814	Thomas Corwin	Ohio	1850
William H. Crawford	Ga	1817	James Guthrie	Ky	1853
Richard Rush	Penn	1825	Howell Cobb	Ga	1857
Samuel D. Ingham	Penn	1829	Philip F. Thomas	Md	1860
Louis McLane	Del	1831	John A. Dix	N. Y	1861
William S. Duane	Penn	1833	Salmon P. Chase	Ohio	1861
Roger B. Taney	Md	1833	Wm P. Fessenden	Me	1864
Levi Woodbury	N. H	1834	Hugh McCullock	Ind	1865
Thomas Ewing	Ohio	1841	George S. Boutwell	Mass	1869

SECRETARIES OF WAR.

Names.	State	When app'd	Names	State	When app'd
Henry Knox	Mass	1789	Joel R. Poinsett	S. C	1837
Timothy Pickering	Penn	1795	John Bell	Tenn	1841
James McHenry	Md	1796	John C. Spencer	N. Y	1841
Samuel Dexter	Mass	1800	James M. Porter	Penn	1843
Roger Griswold	Conn	1801	William Wilkins	Penn	1844
Henry Dearborn	Mass	1801	William L. Marcy	N. Y	1845
William Eustis	Mass	1809	George W. Crawford	Ga	1849
John Armstrong	N. Y	1813	Charles M. Corad	La	1850
James Monroe	Va	1814	Jefferson Davis	Miss	1853
William H. Crawford	Ga	1815	John B. Floyd	Va	1857
George Graham	Va	1817	Joseph Holt	Ky	1860
John C. Calhoun	S. C	1817	Simon Cameron	Penn	1861
James Barbour	Va	1825	Edwin M. Stanton*	Penn	1862
Peter B. Porter	N. Y	1828	John M. Schofield	N. Y	1868
John H. Eaton	Tenn	1829	John A. Rawlins	Ill	1869
Lewis Cass	Mich	1831	William W. Belknap	Iowa	
Benjamin F. Butler	N. Y	1837			

SECRETARIES OF THE NAVY.

Names.	State.	When app'd.	Names	State	When app'd
George Cabot	Mass	1798	Abel P. Upshur	Va	1841
Benjamin Stoddert	Md	1798	David Henshaw	Mass	1843
Robert Smith	Md	1801	Thomas W. Gilmer	Va	1844
Jacob Crowninshield	Mass	1805	John Y. Mason	Va	1844
Paul Hamilton	S. C	1809	George Bancroft	Mass	1845
William Jones	Penn	1813	John Y. Mason	Va	1846
B. W. Crowninshield	Mass	1814	William B. Preston	Va	1849
Smith Thompson	N. Y	1818	William A. Graham	N. C	1850
John Rodgers		1823	John P. Kennedy	Md	1852
Samuel L. Southard	N. J	1823	James C. Dobbin	N. C	1853
John Branch	N. C	1829	Isaac Toucey	Conn	1857
Levi Woodbury	N. H	1831	Gideon Wells	Conn	1861
Mahlon Dickerson	N. J	1834	Adolph E. Borie		1869
James K. Paulding	N. Y	1838	George M. Robeson	N. J	....
George E. Badger	N. C	1841			

POST MASTERS—GENERAL.

Names.	State	When app'd.	Names	State	When app'd
Samuel Osgood	Mass	1799	Jacob Collamer	Vt	1849
Timothy Pickering	Penn	1791	Nathan K. Hall	N. Y	1850
Joseph Habersham	Ga	1795	Samuel D. Hubbard	Conn	1852
Gideon Granger	Conn	1801	James Campbell	Penn	1853
Return Meigs, Jr.	Ohio	1814	Aaron V. Brown	Tenn	1857
John McLean	Ohio	1823	Joseph Holt	Ky	1860
William T. Barry	Ky	1829	Horatio King		1860
Amos Kendall	Ky	1835	Montgomery Blair	Md	1861
John M. Niles	Conn	1840	William Dennison	Ohio	1865
Francis Granger	N. Y	1841	Alex. W. Randall	Wis	1866
Charles A. Wickliffe	Ky	1841	John A. J. Creswell	Md	1869
Cave Johnston	Tenn	1845			

ATTORNEYS-GENERAL.

Names.	State	When app'd	Names	State	When app'd
Edmund Randolph	Va	1789	Hugh S. Legare	S. C	1841
William Bradford	Penn	1794	John Nelson	Md	1843
Charles Lee	Va	1795	John Y. Mason	Va	1845
Levi Lincoln	Mass	1801	Nathan Clifford	Me	1846
Robert Smith	Md	1805	Isaac Toucey	Conn	1848
John Breckenridge	Ky	1805	Reverdy Johnson	Md	2849
Cæsar A. Rodney	Del	1807	John J. Crittendon	Ky	1850
William Pinkney	Md	1811	Caleb Cushing	Mass	1853
Richard Rush	Penn	1814	Jeremiah S. Black	Penn	1857
William Wirt	Va	1817	Edwin M. Stanton	Penn	1860
John M. Berrien	Ga	1829	Edward Bates	Mo	1861
Roger B. Taney	Md	1831	James Speed	Ky	1864
Benjamin F. Butler	N. Y	1833	Henry Stanberry	Ohio	1866
Felix Grundy	Tenn	1838	William M. Evarts	N. Y	1868
Henry D. Gilpin	Penn	1840	E Rockwood Hoar	Mass	1869
John J. Crittenden	Ky	1841	George H. Williams	Ore'n	1869

SECRETARIES OF THE INTERIOR.

Names.	State	When app'p	Names	State	When app'd
Thomas Ewing	Ohio	1849	John P. Usher	Ind	1862
T. M. T. McKennan	Penn	1850	James Harlan	Iowa	1865
Alex'r H. H. Stewart	Va	1850	O. H. Browning	Ill	1866
Robert McClelland	Mich	1853	Jacob D. Coxe	Ohio	1869
Jacob Thompson	Miss	1857	Columbus Delano	Ohio	1869
Caleb B. Smith	Ind	1861			

CHIEF JUSTICES U. S. SUPREME COURT.

John Jay	N. Y	1789	John Marshall	Va	1801
John Rutledge	S. C	1795	Roger B. Taney	Md	1836
Oliver Ellsworth	Conn	1796	Salmon P. Chase	Ohio	1864

ASSOCIATE JUSTICES U. S. SUPREME COURT.

John Rutledge	S. C	1789	Henry Baldwin	Penn	1830
William Cushing	Mass	1789	James M. Wayne	Ga	1835
James Wilson	Penn	1789	Philip P. Barbour	Va	1836
John Blair	Va	1789	John Catron	Tenn	1837
Robert H. Harrison	Md	1789	William Smith	Ala	1837
James Iredell	N. C	1790	John McKinley	Ala	1837
Thomas Johnson	Md	1791	Peter V. Daniel	Va	1841
William Patterson	N. J	1793	Samuel Nelson	N. Y	1845
Samuel Chase	Md	1796	Levi Woodbury	N. H	1845
Bushrod Washington	Va	1798	Robert C. Grier	Penn	1846
Alfred Moore	N. C	1799	Benjamin R. Curtis	Mass	1851
William Johnson	S. C	1804	James A. Campbell	Ala	1853
Brock Livingston	N. Y	1806	Nathan Clifford	Me	1858
Thomas Todd	Ky	1807	Noah H. Swayne	Ohio	1862
Joseph Story	Mass	1811	Samuel F. Miller	Iowa	1862
Gabriel Duval	Md	1811	David Davis	Ill	1862
Smith Thompson	N. Y	1823	Stephen J. Field	Cal	1863
Robert Trimble	Ky	1826	William M. Strong	Pa	....
John McLean	Ohio	1829	Joseph P. Bradley	N. J	....

NAMES OF THE SPEAKERS

OF THE

HOUSE OF REPRESENTATIVES.

From 1789 to 1872.

1st Congress.—FREDERICK AUGUSTUS MUHLENBURGH, of Pennsylvania, was elected speaker of the house of representatives, April 1, 1789, and served to March 3, 1791.

2d Congress.—JONATHAN TRUMBULL, of Connecticut, was elected speaker, and served from the 24th of October, 1791, to March 3, 1793.

3d Congress.—FREDERICK AUGUSTUS MUHLENBURGH, of Pennsylvania, was elected speaker, and served from December 2, 1793, to 3d of March, 1795.

4th and 5th Congresses.—JONATHAN DAYTON, of New Jersey, was elected speaker, and served from 7th of December, 1795, to 3d of March, 1799.

6th Congress.—THEODORE SEDGWICK, of Massachusetts, was elected speaker, and served from 2d December, 1799, to 3d March, 1801.

7th, 8th and 9th Congresses.—NATHANIEL MACON, of North Carolina, was elected speaker, and served from 7th December, 1801, to March 3, 1807.

10th and 11th Congresses.—JOSEPH B. VARNUM, of Massachusetts, was elected speaker, and served from October 26, 1807, to 3d March, 1811.

12th, 13th, 14th, 15th and 16th Congresses.—HENRY CLAY, of Kentucky, was elected speaker, and served from 4th November, 1811, to 3d March, 1821.

17th Congress.—PHILIP P. BARBOUR, of Virginia, was elected speaker, and served from 3d December, 1821, to 3d of March, 1823.

18th *Congress.*—HENRY CLAY, of Kentucky, was elected speaker, and served from 1st of December, 1823, to March 3, 1825.

19th *Congress.*—JOHN W. TAYLOR, of New York, was elected speaker, and served from December 5, 1825, to March 3, 1827.

20th, 21st, 22d and 23d *Congresses.*—ANDREW STEPHENSON, of Virginia, was elected speaker, and served from 3d December, 1827, to 3d of June, 1834; and JOHN BELL, of Tennessee, was, on the 4th of June, 1834, elected to serve out the balance of the 23d Congress, which ended on the 3d of March, 1835.

24th and 25th *Congresses.*—JAMES K. POLK, of Tennessee, was elected speaker, and served from 7th December, 1835, to March 3, 1839.

26th *Congress.*—ROBERT M. T. HUNTER, of Virginia, was elected speaker, and served from the 16th of December, 1839, to March 3, 1841.

27th *Congress.*—JOHN WHITE, of Kentucky, was elected speaker, and served from 31st May, 1841, to March 3, 1843.

28th *Congress.*—JOHN W. JONES, of Virginia, was elected speaker, and served from 4th December 1843, to March 3, 1845.

29th *Congress.*—JOHN W. DAVIS, of Indiana, was elected speaker, and served from 1st December 1845, to March 3, 1847.

30th *Congress.*—ROBERT C. WINTHROP, of Massachusetts, was elected speaker, and served from the 6th of December, 1847, to March 3, 1849.

31st *Congress.*—HOWELL COBB, of Georgia, was elected speaker, and served from 24th December, 1849, to March 3, 1851.

32d and 33d *Congresses.*—LINN BOYD, of Kentucky, was elected speaker, and served from 4th December, 1851, to March 3, 1855.

34th Congress.—NATHANIEL P. BANKS, Jr., of Massachusetts, was elected speaker, and served from February 2, 1856, to March 3, 1857.

35th Congress.—JAMES L. ORR, of South Carolina, was elected speaker, and served from December 7, 1857, to March 3, 1859.

36th Congress.—WILLIAM PENNINGTON, of New Jersey, was elected speaker, February 1, 1860, and served to March 3, 1861.

37th Congress.—GALUSHA A. GROW, of Pennsylvania, was elected speaker, July 4, 1861, and served to March 3, 1863.

38th Congress.—SCHUYLER COLFAX, of Indiana, was elected speaker, December 7, 1863, and served to March 4, 1865.

39th Congress.—SCHUYLER COLFAX, of Indiana, was elected speaker December 4, 1865, and served to March 4, 1867.

40th Congress.—SCHUYLER COLFAX, of Indiana, was elected speaker March 4, 1867, and served to March 4, 1869.

41st Congress.—JAMES G. BLAINE, of Maine, was elected speaker, March 4, 1869, to serve to March 4, 1871.

42d. Congress.—JAMES G. BLAINE, of Maine, was elected speaker, March 4, 1871, to serve to March 4, 1873.

EXISTING GOVERNMENT OF THE UNITED STATES
AND THE
PRINCIPAL OFFICERS THEREIN.
1872.

THE EXECUTIVE.

ULYSSES S. GRANT, of Illinois, *President of the U. States.*
SCHUYLER COLFAX, of Ind., *Vice-President of the U. States.*

THE CABINET.

HAMILTON FISH, of New York, *Secretary of State.*
GEORGE S. BOUTWELL, of Mass., *Secretary of the Treasury.*
WILLIAM W. BELKNAP, of Iowa, *Secretary of War.*
GEORGE M. ROBESON, of New Jersey, *Sec. of the Navy.*
COLUMBUS DELANO, of Ohio, *Secretary of the Interior.*
GEORGE H. WILLIAMS, of Oregon, *Attorney-General.*
JOHN A. J. CRESWELL, of Maryland, *Postmaster-General.*

THE JUDICIARY.
SUPREME COURT OF THE UNITED STATES.

SALMON P. CHASE, of Ohio, *Chief Justice.*
SAMUEL NELSON, of N. Y., *Associate Justice.*
NATHAN CLIFFORD, of Maine, " "
NOAH H. SWAYNE, of Ohio, " "
SAMUEL F. MILLER, of Iowa, " "
DAVID DAVIS, of Illinois, " "
STEPHEN J. FIELD, of Cal., " "
WILLIAM M. STRONG, of Pa., " "
JOSEPH P. BRADLEY, of N. J., " "

Court meets first Monday in December, at Washington.

MINISTERS TO FOREIGN COUNTRIES.
ENVOYS EXTRAORDINARY AND MINISTERS PLENIPOTENTIARY.

Country.	Capital.	Ministers.	State.
Austria	Vienna	John Jay	N. Y.
Brazil	Rio Janeiro	James R. Partridge	Md.
Chili	Santiago	Joseph P. Root	Kan.
China	Pekin	Frederick F. Low	Cal.
France	Paris	Elihu B. Washburne	Ill.
Gt. Britain	London	Robert C. Schenck	Ohio.
Italy	Florence	George P. Marsh	Vt.
Mexico	Mexico	Thomas H. Nelson	Ind.
Peru	Lima	Thomas Settle	N. C.
Germany	Berlin	George Bancroft	Mass.
Russia	St. Petersburg	Andrew G. Curtin	Penn.
Spain	Madrid	Daniel E. Sickles	N. Y.

MINISTERS RESIDENT.

Country	Capital	Minister	State
Argentine Republic	Buenos Ayres		
Belgium	Brussels	J. R. Jones	Ill
Bolivia	Cochabamba	Leopold Markbrett	Ohio
Costa Rica	San Jose	Jacob B. Blair	W. V
Denmark	Copenhagen	M. J. Cramer	Ky
Ecuador	Quito	E. Rumsey Wing	Ky
Guatemala	Guatemala	S. A. Hudson	Iowa
Hawaiian Islands	Honolulu	Henry A. Pierce	Mass
Honduras	Comayagua	Henry Baxter	Mich
Japan	Yedo	C. E. Delong	Ore
Netherlands	Hague	Charles T. Gorham	Mich
Nicaragua	Nicaragua	Charles N. Riotte	Texas
Portugal	Lisbon	Charles H. Lewis	Va
San Salvador	San Salvador	Thomas Biddle	Penn
Sweden and Norway	Stockholm	C. C. Andrews	Mass
Switzerland	Berne	Horace Rublee	Wis
Turkey	Constantinople	George H. Boker	Penn
Uruguay & Paraguay	Montevideo	John L. Stevens	Me
U. S. of Colombia	Bogota	S. A. Hurlburt	Ill
Venezuela	Caracas	William A. Pile	Mo

MINISTERS RESIDENT AND CONSULS GENERAL.

Country	Capital	Minister	State
Hayti	Port-au-Prince	E. D. Bassett	Pa
Liberia	Mourovia	J. Milton Turner	

GOVERNORS OF TERRITORIES.

Territories	Capitols	Governors	Area sq miles	Population
Alaska	Sitka	Not organized	481,276	
Arizona	Tucson	A. P. K. Safford	126,141	9,658
Colorado	Denver	Edward C. McCook	104,500	39,864
Dakota	Yancton	John A. Burbank	142,713	14,181
Dist of Columbia	Washington	Henry D. Cook	60	131,700
Indian Territory	Tahlequah	Cyrus Harris	68,991	
Idaho	Boise	Thomas W. Bennett	90,932	14,999
Montana	Virginia City	Benjamin F. Potts	143,776	20,595
New Mexico	Santa Fe	Marsh Giddings	121,201	91,874
Utah	Salt Lake City	George L. Woods	106,382	86,786
Washington	Olympia	Edward S. Salomon	69,994	23,955
Wyoming	Cheyenne	J. A. Campbell	97,883	9,118

UNITED STATES GOVERNMENT.

JANUARY 1, 1872.

LIST OF MEMBERS OF THE FORTY-SECOND CONGRESS, 1872-3.

SENATE.

SCHUYLER COLFAX, of Indiana, PRESIDENT.
GEORGE C. GORHAM, of California, SECRETARY.

	Term exp.		Term exp.
Alabama.		*Delaware.*	
George E. Spencer	1873	Thomas F. Bayard	1875
George Goldthwaite	1877	Eli Saulsbury	1877
Arkansas.		*Florida.*	
Benjamin F. Rice	1873	Thos. W. Osborn	1873
Powell Clayton	1877	Abijah Gilbert	1875
California.		*Georgia.*	
Cornelius Cole (1)	1873	Joshua Hill	1873
Eugene Casserly	1875	Thos. M. Norwood	1877
Connecticut.		*Illinois.*	
Orris S. Ferry	1873	Lyman Trumbull	1873
W. A. Buckingham	1875	John A. Logan	1877
Indiana.		*Nebraska.*	
Oliver P. Morton	1873	Thomas W. Tipton	1875
Daniel D. Pratt	1875	P. W. Hitchcock	1877
Iowa.		*Nevada.*	
James Harlan	1873	James W. Nye	1873
George G. Wright	1877	William H. Stewart	1875
Kansas.		*New Hampshire.*	
Samuel C. Pomeroy	1873	Jas. W. Patterson	1873
Alex. Caldwell	1877	Aaron H. Cragin	1877
Kentucky.		*New Jersey.*	
Garret Davis (2)	1873	John P. Stockton	1875
Jno. W. Stevenson	1877	F. T. Frelinghuysen	1877

FORTY-SECOND CONGRESS.

	Term exp.		Term exp.
Louisiana.		*New York.*	
William Pitt Kellogg..	1873	Roscoe Conkling.....	1873
Jos. Rodman West....	1877	Reuben E. Fenton....	1875
Maine.		*North Carolina.*	
Hannibal Hamlin.....	1875	John Pool...........	1873
Lot M. Morrill	1877	Z. B. Vance (3)........	1877
Maryland.		*Ohio.*	
George Vickers	1873	John Sherman	1873
Wm. T. Hamilton	1875	Allen G. Thurman....	1875
Massachusetts.		*Oregon.*	
Charles Sumner.......	1875	Henry W. Corbett....	1873
Henry Wilson.........	1877	James K. Kelley	1877
Michigan.		*Pennsylvania.*	
Zachariah Chandler...	1875	Simon Cameron.......	1873
Thomas W. Ferry.....	1877	John Scott	1875
Minnesota.		*Rhode Island.*	
Alexander Ramsay....	1875	William Sprague	1875
William Windom	1877	Henry B. Anthony....	1877
Mississippi.		*South Carolina.*	
Adelbert Ames........	1875	Fred'k A. Sawyer.....	1873
James L. Alcorn	1877	Thos. J. Robertson ...	1877
Missouri.		*Tennessee.*	
Carl Schurz	1875	Wm. G. Brownlow....	1875
Frank P. Blair, Jr	1877	Henry Cooper.........	1877
Texas.		*West Virginia.*	
J. W. Flanagan	1875	Arthur I. Boreman....	1875
M. C. Hamilton	1877	Henry G. Davis	1877
Vermont.		*Wisconsin.*	
Justin S. Morrill	1873	Timothy O. Howe	1873
George F. Edmonds...	1875	Mat. H. Carpenter	1875
Virginia.			
John F. Lewis	1875		
John W. Johnston	1877		

(1) Will be succeeded, in 43d congress, by Aaron A. Sargent, chosen his successor in December, 1871.
(2) Will be succeeded, in 43d congress, by Thomas C. McCreery, chosen his successor in December, 1871.
(3) Not admitted.

HOUSE OF REPRESENTATIVES.

FORTY-SECOND CONGRESS, COMMENCING MARCH 4, 1871, AND ENDING MARCH 4, 1873.

JAMES G. BLAINE, of Maine, SPEAKER.
EDWARD McPHERSON, of Pennsylvania, CLERK.

Alabama — 6.
1. Benjamin S. Turner.
2. Charles W. Buckley.
3. William A. Handley.
4. Charles Hays.
5. Peter M. Dox.
6. Joseph H. Sloss.

Arkansas — 3.
1. James M. Hanks.
2. Oliver P. Snyder.
3. John Edwards.

California — 3.
1. Sherman O. Houghton.
2. Aaron A. Sargent.
3. John M. Coghlan.

Connecticut — 4.
1. Julius D. Strong.
2. Stephen W. Kellogg.
3. Henry H. Starkweather.
4. William H. Barnum.

Delaware — 1.
Benjamin T. Biggs.

Florida — 1.
Josiah T. Walls.

Georgia — 7.
1. Archibald T. McIntyre.
2. Richard H. Whiteley.
3. John S. Bigby.
4. Thomas J. Speer.
5. Dudley M. DuBose.
6. William P. Price.
7. Pierce M. B. Young.

Illinois — 14.
1. Charles B. Farwell.
2. John F. Farnsworth.
3. Horatio C. Burchard.
4. John B. Hawley.
5. Bradford N. Stevens.
6. Henry Snapp.
7. Jesse H. Moore.
8. James C. Robinson.
9. Thompson W. McNeely.
10. Edward Y. Rice.
11. Samuel S. Marshall.
12. John B. Hay.
13. John M. Crebs.

At large, John L. Beveridge.

Indiana — 11.
1. William E. Niblack.
2. Michael C. Kerr.
3. William S. Holman.
4. Jeremiah M. Wilson.
5. John Coburn.
6. Daniel W. Voorhees.
7. Mahlon D. Manson.
8. James N. Tyner.
9. John P. C. Shanks.
10. William Williams.
11. Jasper Packard.

Iowa — 6.
1. George W. McCrary.
2. Aylett R. Cotton.
3. William G. Donnan.
4. Madison M. Walden.
5. Frank W. Palmer.
6. Jackson Orr.

Kansas — 1.
David P. Lowe.

FORTY-SECOND CONGRESS.

Kentucky — 9.
1. Edward Crossland.
2. Henry D. McHenry.
3. Joseph H. Lewis.
4. William B. Read.
5. Boyd Winchester.
6. William E. Arthur.
7. James B. Beck.
8. George M. Adams.
9. John M. Rice.

Louisiana — 5.
1. J. Hale Sypher.
2. Lionel A. Sheldon.
3. Chester B. Darrall.
4.
5. Frank Morey.

Maine — 5.
1. John Lynch.
2. William P. Frye.
3. James G. Blaine.
4. John A. Peters.
5. Eugene Hale.

Maryland — 5.
1. Samuel Hambleton.
2. Stevenson Archer.
3. Thomas Swann.
4. John Ritchie.
5. William M. Merrick.

Massachusetts — 10.
1. James Buffinton.
2. Oakes Ames.
3. Ginery Twichell.
4. Samuel Hooper.
5. Benjamin F. Butler.
6. Nathaniel P. Banks.
7. George M. Brooks.
8. George F. Hoar.
9.
10. Henry L. Dawes.

Michigan — 6.
1. Henry Waldron.
2. William L. Stoughton.
3. Austin Blair.
4. Wilder D. Foster.
5. Omar D. Conger.
6. Jabez G. Sutherland.

Minnesota — 2.
1. Mark H. Dunnell.
2. John T. Averill.

Mississippi — 5.
1. George E. Harris.
2. Joseph L. Morphis.
3. Henry W. Barry.
4. George C. McKee.
5. Legrand W. Perce.

Missouri — 9.
1. Erastus Wells.
2. Gustavus A. Finkelnburg.
3. James R. McCormick.
4. Harrison E. Havens.
5. Samuel S. Burdett.
6. Abram Comingo.
7. Isaac C. Parker.
8. James G. Blair.
9. Andrew King.

Nebraska — 1.
John Taffe.

Nevada — 1.
Charles W. Kendall.

New Hampshire — 3
1. Ellery A. Hibbard.
2. Samuel N. Bell.
3. Hosea W. Parker.

New Jersey — 5.
1. John W. Hazelton.
2. Samuel C. Forker.
3. John T. Bird.
4. John Hill.
5. George A. Halsey.

New York — 31.
1. Dwight Townsend.
2. Thomas Kinsella.
3. Henry W. Slocum.
4. Robert B. Roosevelt.
5. William R. Roberts.
6. Samuel S. Cox.
7. Smith Ely, Jr.
8. James Brooks.
9. Fernando Wood.
10. Clarkson N. Potter.

FORTY-SECOND CONGRESS.

11. Charles St. John.
12. John H. Ketcham.
13. Joseph H. Tuthill.
14. Eli Perry.
15. Joseph M. Warren.
16. John Rogers.
17. William A. Wheeler.
18. John M. Carroll.
19. Elizur H. Prindle.
20. Clinton L. Merriam.
21. Ellis H. Roberts.
22. William E. Lansing.
23. R. Holland Duell.
24. John R. Seeley.
25. William H. Lamport.
26. Milo Goodrich.
27. Horace Boardman Smith.
28. Freeman Clarke.
29. Seth Wakeman.
30. William Williams.
31. Walter L. Sessions.

North Carolina — 7.

1. Clinton L. Cobb.
2. Charles R. Thomas.
3. Alfred M. Waddell.
4.
5. James M. Leach.
6. Francis E. Shober.
7. James C. Harper.

Ohio — 19.

1. Aaron F. Perry.
2. Job E. Stevenson.
3. Lewis D. Campbell.
4. John F. McKinney.
5. Charles N. Lamison.
6. John A. Smith.
7. Samuel Shellabarger.
8. John Beatty.
9. Charles Foster.
10. Erasmus D. Peck.
11. John T. Wilson.
12. Philadelph Van Trump.
13. George W. Morgan.
14. James Munroe.
15. William P. Sprague.
16. John A. Bingham.
17. Jacob A. Ambler.
18. William H. Upson.
19. James A. Garfield.

Oregon — 1.

James H. Slater.

Pennsylvania — 24.

1. Samuel J. Randall.
2. John V. Creely.
3. Leonard Myers.
4. William D. Kelley.
5. Alfred C. Harmer.
6. Ephraim L. Acker.
7. Washington Townsend.
8. J. Lawrence Getz.
9. Oliver J. Dickey.
10. John W. Killinger.
11. John B. Storm.
12. Lazarus D. Shoemaker.
13. Ulysses Mercur.
14. John B. Packer.
15. Richard J. Haldeman.
16. Benjamin F. Meyers.
17. R. Milton Speer.
18. Henry Sherwood.
19. Glenni W. Scofield.
20. Samuel Griffith.
21. Henry D. Foster.
22. James S. Negley.
23. Ebenezer McJunkin.
24. William McClelland.

Rhode Island — 2.

1. Benjamin T. Eames.
2. James M. Pendleton.

South Carolina — 4.

1. Joseph H. Rainey.
2. Robert C. DeLarge.
3. Robert B. Elliott.
4. Alexander S. Wallace.

Tennessee — 8.

1. Roderick R. Butler.
2. Horace Maynard.
3. Abraham E. Garrett.
4. John M. Bright.
5. Edward I. Golladay.
6. W. C. Whitthorne.
7. Robert P. Caldwell.
8. William W. Vaughan.

Texas — 4.

1. William S. Herndon.

2. John C. Conner.
3.
4. John Hancock.

Vermont — 3.
1. Charles W. Willard.
2. Luke P. Poland.
3. Worthington C. Smith.

Virginia — 8.
1. John Critcher.
2. James H. Platt, Jr.
3. Charles H. Porter.
4. William H. H. Stowell.
5. Richard T. W. Duke.
6. John T. Harris.
7. Elliott M. Braxton.
8. William Terry.

West Virginia — 3.
1. John J. Davis.
2. James G. McGrew.
3. Frank Hereford.

Wisconsin — 6.
1. Alexander Mitchell.
2. Gerry W. Hazelton.
3. J. Allen Barber.
4. Charles A. Eldridge.
5. Philetus Sawyer.
6. Jeremiah M. Rusk.

TERRITORIAL DELEGATES.

Arizona.
Richard C. McCormick.

Colorado.
Jerome B. Chaffee.

Dakota.
Moses K. Armstrong.

District of Columbia.
Norton P. Chipman.

Idaho.
Samuel A. Merritt.

Montana.
William H. Clagett.

New Mexico.

Utah.
William H. Hooper.

Washington.
Selucius Garfielde.

Wyoming.
William T. Jones.

GOVERNMENTS OF THE SEVERAL STATES.

1872.

States	Capitals	Governors	Terms Expire	Salaries
Alabama	Montgomery	*Robert B. Lindsay*	Nov 1872	$4,000
Arkansas	Little Rock	O. A. Hadley*	Jan 1873	5,000
California	Sacramento	Newton Booth	Dec 1875	7,000
Connecticut	Hfd & N. H	Marshall Jewell	May 1873	2,000
Delaware	Dover	*James Ponder*	Jan 1875	1,333
Florida	Tallahassee	Harrison Reed	Jan 1873	1,500
Georgia	Atlanta	*James Milton Smith*	Jan 1873	4,000
Illinois	Springfield	John W. Palmer	Jan 1873	1,500
Indiana	Indianapolis	Conrad Baker	Jan 1873	3,000
Iowa	Des Moines	Cyrus C. Carpenter	Jan 1874	2,500
Kansas	Topeka	James M. Harvey	Jan 1873	2,000
Kentucky	Frankfort	*Preston H. Leslie*	Sept 1874	5,000
Louisiana	New Orleans	Henry C. Warmoth	Jan 1873	8,000
Maine	Augusta	Sydney Perham	Jan 1873	2,500
Maryland	Annapolis	*Wm. Pinckney Whyte*	Jan 1876	3,600
Massachusetts	Boston	Wm. D. Washburn	Jan 1873	5,000
Michigan	Lansing	Henry P. Baldwin	Jan 1873	1,500
Minnesota	St. Paul	Horace Austin	Jan 1874	3,000
Mississippi	Jackson	Ridgley C. Powers*	Jan 1874	3,000
Missouri	Jefferson City	B. Gratz Brown†	Jan 1873	2,500
Nebraska	Lincoln	William H. James*	Jan 1873	1,200
Nevada	Carson City	L. R. Bradley	Jan 1871	6,000
New Hampshire	Concord	Ezekiel A. Straw	June 1873	1,000
New Jersey	Trenton	*Joel Parker*	Jan 1875	3,000
New York	Albany	John T. Hoffman	Jan 1873	4,000
North Carolina	Raleigh	T. R. Caldwell*	Jan 1873	5,000
Ohio	Columbus	Edward F. Noyes	Jan 1874	4,000
Oregon	Salem	L. F. Grover	Sept 1874	1,500
Pennsylvania	Harrisburg	John W. Geary	Jan 1873	5,000
Rhode Island	N'port & Prov	Seth Padelford	May 1873	1,000
South Carolina	Columbia	Robert K. Scott	Jan 1873	4,000
Tennessee	Nashville	*John C. Brown*	Oct 1874	3,000
Texas	Austin	Edmund J. Davis	Nov 1873	5,000
Vermont	Montpelier	John W. Stewart	Oct 1872	1,000
Virginia	Richmond	Gilbert C. Walker	Jan 1874	5,000
West Virginia	Charleston	John J. Jacob	Mar 1874	2,000
Wisconsin	Madison	C. C. Washburn	Jan 1874	1,250

Democrats in Italic. *Ex-Officers. †Liberal Republicans.

GOVERNMENTS OF THE SEVERAL STATES.
(CONTINUED.)

States	Area. sq miles	Population. 1870	Legislatures Meet	State Elections
Alabama	50,722	996,992	3 M Nov	Tu aft 1 M Nov
Arkansas	52,198	484,471	1 M Jan	1 Monday Nov
California	188,981	560,247	*1 M Dec	1 Wed Sept
Connecticut	4,750	537,454	1 W May	1 Monday April
Delaware	2,120	125,015	*1 Tu Jan	1 Tuesday Aug
Florida	59,248	187,748	T a 1 M Jan	Tu aft 1 M Nov
Georgia	58,000	1,184,109	*1 W Jan	Tu aft 1 M Nov
Illinois	55,410	2,539,891	*1 M Jan	Tu aft 1 M Nov
Indiana	33,809	1,680,637	*1 W Jan	2 Tuesday Oct
Iowa	55,045	1,191,792	*2 M Jan	2 Tuesday Oct
Kansas	81,318	364,399	2 Tu Jan	Tu aft 1 M Nov
Kentucky	37,680	1,321,011	*1 M Dec	1 Monday Aug
Louisiana	41,346	726,915	1 M Jan	1 Monday Nov
Maine	35,000	626,915	1 W Jan	2 Monday Sept
Maryland	11,124	780,894	*1 W Jan	Tu aft 1 M Nov
Massachusetts	7,800	1,457,351	W Jan	Tu aft 1 M Nov
Michigan	56,451	1,184,059	*1 W Jan	Tu aft 1 M Nov
Minnesota	83,531	439,706	T a 1 M Jan	Tu aft 1 M Nov
Mississippi	47,156	827,922	T a 1 M Jan	Tu aft 1 M Nov
Missouri	65,350	1,721,295	*Last M Dec	Tu aft 1 M Nov
Nebraska	75,995	122,993	*Th a 1 M Jan	2 Tuesday Oct
Nevada	81,531	42,491	*1 M Jan	Tu aft 1 M Nov
New Hampshire	9,280	318,300	1 M June	2 Tuesday Mar
New Jersey	8,320	906,096	2 Tu Jan	Tu aft 1 M Nov
New York	47,000	4,382,758	1 Tu Jan	Tu aft 1 M Nov
North Carolina	50,704	1,071,361	1 Th Nov	1 Thursday Aug
Ohio	30,964	2,665,260	*1 M Jan	2 Tuesday Oct
Oregon	95,274	90,923	2 M Sept	2 Monday June
Pennsylvania	46,000	3,521,791	1 Tu Jan	2 Tuesday Oct
Rhode Island	1,306	217,353	May & Jan	1 Wed April
South Carolina	34,000	705,606	3 W Oct	4 Monday Nov
Tennessee	45,600	1,258,520	*1 M Oct	1 Monday Aug
Texas	274,356	818,579	2 Tu Jan	1 Tuesday Nov
Vermont	10,212	330,051	*2 Th Oct	1 Tuesday Sept
Virginia	38,352	1,225,168	1 M Dec	Tu aft 1 M Nov
West Virginia	23,000	442,014	2 Tu Jan	4 Thursday Oct
Wisconsin	53,924	1,054,670	1 W Jan	Tu aft 1 M Nov

*Biennial Sessions and Elections.

RESULTS AT THE LATEST STATE ELECTIONS
1871—1872.

MAINE.—Total vote for Governor, 106,908; viz; Sidney Perham, Rep. 58,757; Kimball, Dem. 48126; scattering 25· Perham over Kimball, 10,631; over all, 10,606.
Republican majority on Joint Ballot in Legislature, 96.

NEW HAMPSHIRE.—Total vote for Governor, 76,372; viz; Ezekiel A. Straw, Rep. 38,752; Democratic candidate, 36,586; Balance were scattering. Straw over Democratic candidate, 2,166; over all others, 1,132.
Republican majority on Joint Ballot in Legislature, 62.

VERMONT.—John W. Stewart the Republican candidate for Governor, received 33,367 votes, being a majority of 21,309 over the Democratic candidate.
Republican majority on Joint Ballot 203.

MASSACHUSETTS.—Total vote for Governor, 136,793; viz; William B. Washburn Rep. 75,129; Adams, Dem. 47,775; the rest scattering. Washburn over Adams, 27,404; over all, 13,465.
Republican majority on Joint Ballot in Legislature, 142.

CONNECTICUT.—Total vote for Governor, 93,098, viz; Marshall Jewell, Rep. 46,563; Dem. 44,562; scattering 1,973 Jewell over Hubbard, Dem. 2,001; over all, 28.
Republican majority on Joint Ballot, 28.

RHODE ISLAND.—Seth Padelford the Republican candidate for Governor received 9,456 against 8,280, for the Democratic candidate, being a majority of 1,132.
Republican majority on Joint Ballot in the Legislature, 48.

NEW YORK.—Total vote in 1870, for *Governor,* 769,354, viz;

John T. Hoffman, Dem. 399,552; Stewart L. Woodford Rep. 366,436. Rest scattering. Hoffman over Woodford, 33,116.
Total vote in 1871 for *Secretary of State*, 757,151, viz; Scribner; Rep. 387,119; Willers, Dem. 368,212. Scribner over Willers 18,007.
Republican majority on Joint Ballot in Legislature, 82.

NEW JERSEY.—Total vote in 1871 for Governor, 158,745, viz; Joel Parker, Dem. 82,302; Cornelius Walsh, Rep. 76,383. Parker over Walsh, 5,079.
Republican majority on Joint Ballot in Legislature, 15.

PENNSYLVANIA.—Total vote in 1871 for Auditor-General, 556,805 viz; David Stanton, Rep. 284,097—Wilson McCandless, Dem. 269,522. Balance were scattering. Stanton over McCandless, 14,575.
Republican majority on Joint Ballot 23.

DELAWARE.—James Ponder, the Democratic candidate for Governor, received 12,458 against 9,982 for the Democratic candidate, being a majority of 2,476.
Democratic majority on Joint Ballot in the Legislature, 30.

MARYLAND.—Total vote in 1871 for Governor, 132,783 viz; William P. Whyte, Dem. 73,959; Jacob Tome, Rep. 58,824. Whyte over Tome 15,135.
Democratic majority in the Legislature, 81.

VIRGINIA.—Elected a Legislature in 1871, strongly Conservative, which means Democratic in that State. For Governor: Walker, Conservative, received 119,535 against 101,204 Rep. Democratic majority, 18,331.
Democratic majority in the Legislature 90.

WEST VIRGINIA.—In 1871, at an election for a Constitutional Convention; Republican vote stood, 27,688—Democratic, 30,539. Democratic majority, 2,857, they voting for it.
Democratic majority in the Legislature on Joint Ballot, 56.

STATE ELECTIONS.

NORTH CAROLINA.—In 1871, at an election for a convention to revise the Constitution, the Republican vote against it was 95,352; the Democratic vote for it was 86,007—Republican majority 9,345.
Republican majority on Joint Ballot in Legislature, 5.

SOUTH CAROLINA.—At the last election the, vote stood Rep. 85,071 against 51,537 Dem. Republican majority 33,534.
Republican majority on Joint Ballot in Legislature, 98.

GEORGIA.—In 1871, at an election to fill the vacancy for Governor, James Milton Smith, Dem. received 96,685, against 69,822—Democratic majority, 26,863.
Democratic majority on Joint Ballot in Legislature, 127.

FLORIDA.—Congressional vote, 1870—Dem. 13,438; Rep. 13,206; no election for State officer since 1868.
Legislature largely Democratic.

ALABAMA.—At the last election, Democratic vote was 79,447, against 77,676, Republican.
Democratic majority on Joint Ballot in Legislature, 9.

MISSISSIPPI.—In 1871, this State voted for Legislature, and County Offices. For District Attorney, the vote stood, for Republican candidate, 83,102, against 59,053 for the Democratic candidate.

Republican majority on Joint Ballot in Legislature, 21.

LOUISIANA.—At last election, the State was Rep. 65,647; Dem. 41,170—Republican majority, 24,447.
Republican majority on Joint Ballot in Legislature, 70.

TEXAS.—Congressional vote in 1871, was 125,812, and the Democratic majority was about 24,000. For Governor in 1869 Davis, Rep. had a majority of 338 over all others.
Republican majority on Joint Ballot in Legislature, 9.

OHIO.—Total vote in 1871, for Governor, 460,462, viz; Edward F. Noyes, Rep. 238,273; McCook, Dem. 218,105; the rest scattering. Noyes over McCook 20,168; over all 16,084.
Republican majority on Joint Ballot in Legilature, 9.

INDIANA.—The vote for Secretary of State, was 160,059. Democratic, against 157,491, Republican. Democratic majority, 2,568.
Democratic majority on Joint Ballot in Legislature, 4.

ILLINOIS.—An election was held in 1871, for Congressman at Large in place of John A. Logan—Total vote 253,263; viz; John L. Beveridge, Rep. 137,926; Hayes, Dem. 115,337. Beveridge over Hayes 22,589.
Republican majority on Joint Ballot in the Legislature, 55.

KENTUCKY.—Total vote in 1871 for Governor, 215,741; viz; Preston H. Leslie, Dem. 126,447; J. M. Harlan, Rep. 89,294. Leslie over Harlan, 37,153.
Democratic majority on Joint Ballot in Legislature, 79.

TENNESSEE.—At the last election, the vote stood 78,979 Democratic, against 41,500 Republican.
Democratic majority on Joint Ballot in Legislature, 70.

MICHIGAN.—Total vote 183,670 of which there was Rep. 100,176; Dem.83,494; Republican majority 16,682.
Republican majority on Joint Ballot in the Legislature, 67.

WISCONSIN.—Vote for Governor 1871—Total 147,269; viz; Cadwallader C. Washburne, Rep. 78,299; James R. Doolittle, Dem. 68,970. Washburne over Doolittle 9,329.
Republican majority on Joint Ballot in Legislature, 29.

IOWA.—Election in 1871 for Supreme Court Judge—Total vote 176,348, viz; James G. Day, Rep. 108,801; John F. Duncombe, Dem. 67,547. Day over Duncombe, 41,254.
Republican majority on Joint Ballot in the Legislature, 90.

STATE ELECTIONS.

MISSOURI.—Vote for B. Gratz Brown, Liberal Republican 104,374, against the opposition candidate. Brown's majority, 41,038.
Democratic majority on Joint Ballot in Legislature, 6.

ARKANSAS.—Republican vote, 30,574; Democratic, 25,690, Republican majority, 4,884.
Republican majority on Joint Ballot in Legislature, 48.

CALIFORNIA.—Total vote in 1871 for Governor, 120,101; viz; Newton Booth, Rep. 62,581; Henry H. Haight, Dem. 57,520. Booth over Haight, 5,061.
Republican majority on Joint Ballot in the Legislature, 26.

MINNESOTA.—Total vote in 1871 for Governor, 77,856; viz; Horace Austin, Rep. 46,415; Winthrop Young, Dem. 31,441. Austin over Young, 14,974.
Republican majority on Joint Ballot in the Legislature, 55.

OREGON.—Democratic vote in this State, was 11,726, against 11,025 Republican. Democratic majority 631.
Democratic majority in the Legislature, 25.

KANSAS.—Republican vote in this State, was 40,666, against 20,496 Democrat; Republican majority 20,170.
Republican majoirty on Joint Ballot in Legislature, 75.

NEVADA.—Total vote for Governor, in 1870, 13,347; viz; Bradley, Dem. 7,200; Tritte, Rep. 6,147. Bradley over Tritte 1,053.
Democratic majority on Joint Ballot in Legislature, 4.

NEBRASKA.—Total vote in 1870 for Governor, 19,774; viz; David Butler, Rep. 11,126; J H. Croxton, Dem. 8,648. Butler over Croxton 2,478.
Republican majority on Joint Ballot in the Legislature, 26.

WASHINGTON'S ADMINISTRATION,

WITH

BIOGRAPHICAL SKETCH.
1789—1797.

TWO TERMS—EIGHT YEARS.

ELECTED BY THE UNANIMOUS VOTE OF THE ELECTORS.

CABINET.

PRESIDENT:
George Washington, Virginia.

VICE-PRESIDENT:
John Adams, Massachusetts.

SECRETARIES OF STATE:
Thomas Jefferson, Virginia.	1789.
Edmund Randolph, Virginia.	1794.
Timothy Pickering, Massachusetts.	1795.

SECRETARIES OF THE TREASURY:
Alexander Hamilton, New York.	1789.
Oliver Wolcott, Connecticut.	1795.

SECRETARIES OF WAR AND NAVY:
Henry Knox, Massachusetts.	1789.
Timothy Pickering, Massachusetts.	1794.
James McHenry, Maryland.	1796.

POSTMASTERS-GENERAL:
Samuel Osgood, Massachusetts.	1789.
Timothy Pickering, Massachusetts.	1794.
Joseph Habersham, Georgia.	1795.

ATTORNEYS-GENERAL:
Edmund Randolph, Virginia.	1789.
William Bradford, Pennsylvania.	1794.
Charles Lee, Virginia.	1795.

FINANCIAL CONDITION OF THE COUNTRY.

Year	Imports	Exports	Expenditures	Debt
1790	$23,000,000	$20,205,156	....	$75,463,476
1791	29,200,000	19,012,041	$7,207,539	77,227,924
1792	31,500,000	20,753,098	9,141,569	80,352,634
1793	31,000,000	26,109,572	7,529,575	78,427,404
1794	34,600,000	33,026,233	9,302,124	80,747,587
1795	69,756,268	47,989,472	10,405,069	83,762,172
1796	81,436,164	67,064,097	8,367,776	

GEORGE WASHINGTON.

BIOGRAPHICAL SKETCH.

The twenty-second day of February 1732, will ever be memorable, as the birthday of that great and good man who has been justly styled the "Father of his country." Descended from English ancestors, who emigrated to this country, and settled in Virginia as early as 1657, he was born in a plain farm-house upon the banks of the Potomac, in the County of Westmoreland, Va., on the day above mentioned.

GEORGE WASHINGTON.

His father, Augustine Washington, died in 1743, when George —who was his eldest son by his second wife, Mary Ball—was but ten years of age. He was blessed with a kind, affectionate and intelligent mother, by whom he was instructed in sound principles and correct habits.

At the early age of fifteen, an opportunity was afforded him of entering the British Navy as a midshipman, which position he strongly desired as a path to honorable distinction, but the evident reluctance of his mother to the separation induced him to abandon the project.

He received a good English, but not a thorough literary or scientific education. Having a mind naturally philosophical and mathematical, his attention was given to surveying, and to the science of arms; and of athletic exercises he was passionately fond. At the age of nineteen, he was appointed one of the Adjutant-Generals of Virginia with the rank of Major.

In October 1753, he was commissioned by Governor Dinwidde of Virginia to convey important dispatches to the French on the Ohio, which hazardous undertaking, after suffering great hardships and escaping many dangers, he accomplished to the great satisfaction of the Governor. Subsequently, in 1754, he was appointed Lieutenant-Colonel, and under Colonel Fry was sent with a regiment of troops against the French, and having received permission to march with two companies in advance, on the dark and rainy night of May 24th, 1754, he surrounded and surprised a detachment of French troops, who were compelled to surrender.

This was the commencement of his glorious military career, the history of which is familiar to every American citizen. After his return from the successful expedition against the French in 1758, and the close of the Campaign, he left the army, and was married to a Mrs. Martha Custis, a widow lady of Virginia, who was highly esteemed for her amiable disposition and womanly virtues.

During the subsequent sixteen years, he devoted his time principally in the cultivation of his estate, and in the enjoyment of domestic life at Mount Vernon. In 1774, he represented Virginia as a delegate in the Continental Congress, and on the 15th of June, 1775, was unanimously appointed Commander-in Chief of the American forces, which position he held till the close of the war.

In May 1787, he was a delegate to the Convention which met at Philadelphia, and was appointed to preside over the same, and exerted his influence to cause the adoption of the Constitution.

Having been unanimously elected the first President of the United States, the inauguration ceremonies took place on the 30th of April, 1789, in the City Hall in the city of New York. The first session of the first Congress, held at New York, occupied a period of six months, the adjournment taking place on the 29th of September 1789. In 1793, he was unanimously re-elected to the presidency for another term by the two great political parties, who united only on the name of Washington. Having determined to retire from office, he issued in 1796 his farewell address to the people of the United States, so full of love, and wisdom, and anxiety for the future welfare of his country, and in 1797, after witnessing the inauguration of his successor, he retired to Mount Vernon to spend the rest of his days in retirement.

His administration was a wise and successful one; all disputes with foreign nations had been adjusted, excepting those of France. Ample provision had been made for the security and ultimate payment of the public debt; public and private credit had been restored, and the affairs of the country were prosperous.

On Thursday, the 12th of December, 1799, he was seized with an inflammation in his throat, and on the 14th of the same month, he died, in the sixty-eighth year of his age.

ADAMS'S ADMINISTRATION,

WITH

BIOGRAPHICAL SKETCH.
1797–1801.

ONE TERM—FOUR YEARS.

ELECTED BY THE FEDERALISTS.

CABINET.

PRESIDENT:
JOHN ADAMS, Massachusetts.

VICE-PRESIDENT:
THOMAS JEFFERSON, Virginia.

SECRETARIES OF STATE:
TIMOTHY PICKERING, Massachusetts. 1797.
JOHN MARSHALL, Virginia. 1797.

SECRETARIES OF THE TREASURY:
OLIVER WOLCOTT, Connecticut. 1797.
SAMUEL DEXTER, Massachusetts. 1800.

SECRETARIES OF WAR:
JAMES MCHENRY, Maryland. 1797.
SAMUEL DEXTER, Massachusetts. 1800.
ROGER GRISWOLD, Connecticut. 1801.

SECRETARIES OF THE NAVY:
GEORGE CABOT, Massachusetts. 1798.
BENJAMIN STODDERT, Maryland. 1798.

POST MASTER GENERAL:
JOSEPH HABERSHAM, Georgia. 1797.

ATTORNEY-GENERAL:
CHARLES LEE, Virginia. 1797.

FINANCIAL CONDITION OF THE COUNTRY.

Year	Imports	Exports	Expenditures	Debt
1797	$75,379,406	$56,850,206	$8,626,012	$82,064,479
1798	68,551,700	61,527,097	8,613,507	79,228,529
1799	79,089,148	78,665,522	11,077,043	78,408,669
1800	91,252,768	70,970,780	11,989,739	82,976,291

JOHN ADAMS.

BIOGRAPHICAL SKETCH.

John Adams, the second President of the United States, was the fourth in descent from Henry Adams, who fled from persecution in England, and settled in Massachusetts in the year 1630. He was born on the 19th of October, 1735, in the town of Braintree, Massachusetts, and in 1751, was admitted a member of Harvard College, graduating therefrom four years afterwards.

He soon after commenced the study of law at Worcester,

JOHN ADAMS.

Massachusetts, supporting himself chiefly by teaching in one of the public schools of that town. He was admitted to the bar of Suffolk County in 1758, and in 1766, he removed to Boston, where he soon distinguished himself in his profession.

In 1764, he married Abigail Smith, daughter of Rev. William

Smith, of Weymouth, an educated lady, possessing superior intellectual faculties.

Having filled many important offices, he was in 1777, appointed a commissioner to the Court of France, and in 1779, was appointed a Minister Plenipotentiary for negotiating a treaty of peace with Great Britain. In 1781, he was associated with Franklin, Jay, and others in a commission for concluding treaties of peace with the several European powers. In 1784, he was in Holland and France, negotiating commercial treaties with foreign nations. In 1785, he was appointed by Congress a Minister to represent the United States at the Court of Great Britain.

He resigned in 1788, and in June returned to the United States, after an absence of over eight years.

Ability, coupled with *public honesty* and *private worth*, constitute a man equal to any emergency, and fitted for any public position. Adams possessed this character, and these qualifications in an eminent degree. He was the man for the times; no purer patriot ever lived; he was the eloquent and fearless defender of the Declaration of Independence. He was a patriot and a scholar.

He was elected to the Presidency as the successor of Washington after a close and spirited contest, in which his warm personal friend, Thomas Jefferson, was his principle rival. Mr. Jefferson was supported by the Democratic, then called the Republican party, and Mr. Adams by the Federal party. Mr. Jefferson was elected Vice-President.

His inauguration took place in Congress Hall, Philadelphia, on the 4th of March, 1797, he being then in his sixty-second year. He served his term of four years, was again nominated, but defeated. After his term of service had expired, he retired to his estate at Quincy, Massachusetts, and passed the remainder of his days in literary and scientific pursuits. Having lived to the good old age of *ninety-one years*, he died on the 4th of July 1826.

JEFFERSON'S ADMINISTRATION,

WITH

BIOGRAPHICAL SKETCH.
1801–1809.

TWO TERMS—EIGHT YEARS.

ELECTED BY THE REPUBLICAN OR ANTI FEDERAL PARTY.

CABINET.

PRESIDENT:
Thomas Jefferson, Virginia.

VICE-PRESIDENTS:
Aaron Burr, New York.	1801.
George Clinton, New York.	1805.

SECRETARY OF STATE:
James Madison, Virginia. 1801.

SECRETARIES OF THE TREASURY:
Samuel Dexter, Massachusetts.	1801.
Albert Gallatin, Pennsylvania.	1802.

SECRETARY OF WAR:
Henry Dearborn, Massachusetts. 1801.

SECRETARIES OF THE NAVY:
Benjamin Stoddert, Maryland.	1801.
Robert Smith, Maryland.	1802.
Jacob Crowninshield, Mass.	1805.

POST MASTERS-GENERAL:
Joseph Habersham, Georgia.	1801.
Gideon Granger, Connecticut.	1802.

ATTORNEYS-GENERAL:
Theophilus Parsons, Massachusetts	1801.
Levi Lincoln, Massachusetts.	1801.
Robert Smith, Maryland.	1805.
John Breckenridge, Kentucky.	1805.
Cæsar A. Rodney, Delaware.	1807.

FINANCIAL CONDITION OF THE COUNTRY.

Year.	Imports.	Exports.	Expenditures.	Debt.
1801	$111,363,511	$94,115,925	$12,273,376	$83,038,050
1802	76,333,333	72,483,160	13,276,084	80,712,632
1803	64,666,666	55,800,038	11,258,983	77,054,686
1804	185,000,000	77,699,074	12,624,646	86,427,120
1805	130,600,000	95,566,021	13,727,124	82,312,150
1806	129,410,000	101,536,963	15,070,093	75,723,270
1807	138,500,000	108,343,151	11,292,292	69,218,398
1808	56,990,000	22,430,960	16,764,584	65,196,317

THOMAS JEFFERSON.

BIOGRAPHICAL SKETCH.

Perhaps the most distinguished statesman this country has ever produced, was Thomas Jefferson, the third President of the United States. His ancestors were also early emigrants from Great Britain, who settled in Virginia. His father, Peter Jefferson, was a man of some distinction in the colony.

Thomas Jefferson was born on the 2nd of April, 1743, at Shadwell, in Albemarle County, Virginia. His father dying when he was twelve years of age, left him a large inheritance.

THOMAS JEFFERSON.

He was educated at the College of William and Mary, studied law under the celebrated George Wythe, and commenced its practice in 1767.

He was early identified with the champions of liberty, and in 1775, took his seat in the Continental Congress. Previous to this, he had made an effort in the Legislature of which he was a member, for the emancipation of the slaves in Virginia, but was unsuccessful. In 1772, he married Mrs. Martha Skelton, a widow lady, daughter of Mr. John Wyles, an eminent lawyer of Virginia.

Although one of the youngest members of the Continental Congress, he was selected by a committee duly appointed, and requested to prepare the *Declaration* of *Independence*. This he did, and it was finally adopted with but few alterations and amendments on the 4th of July, 1776. In 1779, he was elected Governor of Virginia, which office he held for two years. He was the author of many tracts, and other writings, and as a man of letters acquired high distinction.

In 1785, he was joined with Adams and Franklin in a commission for negotiating treaties of commerce with foreign nations, and he met them in Paris, in June of that year, and it was through him, as Mr. Webster has confessed, that our diplomatic intercourse was raised to a dignity and strength, which will bear comparison with any that other governments can produce.

Having been elected President his inauguration took place in the new Capitol at Washington, on the 4th of March, 1801 in the 58th year of his age. He was elected by the Anti-Federal or Democratic party, and many important acts were passed and many important events took place during his administration which was continued for eight years (he having been re-elected in 1805). He almost doubled the territory of the Union; caused the vast regions of the West to be explored; gave us character abroad, and tranquility at home.

Having retired from the presidency, he passed the remainder of his days in the cultivation of his beautiful estate at Monticello; in pleasant intercourse with his friends; in literary pursuits, and in advancing his favorite project of a University of Virginia. His pecuniary circumstances becoming embarrassed in his old age, he was compelled to dispose of his library, which was purchased by Congress for $23,950. He died, after a short illness, on the 4th of July, 1826, being the fiftieth aniversary of our Independence; the same day that his friend and compatriot John Adams departed this life.

MADISON'S ADMINISTRATION,

WITH

BIOGRAPHICAL SKETCH.
1809–1817.

TWO TERMS—EIGHT YEARS.

ELECTED BY THE REPUBLICANS [ANTI-FEDERALISTS.]

CABINET.

PRESIDENT:
JAMES MADISON, Virginia.

VICE-PRESIDENTS:
GEORGE CLINTON, New York.
ELBRIDGE GERRY, Massachusetts.

SECRETARIES OF STATE:
ROBERT SMITH, Maryland.	1809.
JAMES MONROE, Virginia.	1811.

SECRETARIES OF THE TREASURY.
ALBERT GALLATIN, Pennsylvania.	1809.
GEORGE W. CAMPBELL, Tennessee.	1814.
ALEXANDER J. DALLAS, Penn.	1814.

SECRETARIES OF WAR:
WILLIAM EUSTIS, Massachusetts.	1809.
JOHN ARMSTRONG, New York.	1813.
JAMES MONROE, Virginia.	1814.
WILLIAM H. CRAWFORD, Georgia.	1815.

SECRETARIES OF THE NAVY:
PAUL HAMILTON, South Carolina.	1809.
WILLIAM JONES, Pennsylvania.	1813.
BENJAMIN W. CROWINSHIELD, Mass.	1814.

POSTMASTERS-GENERAL.
GIDEON GRANGER, Connecticut.	1809.
RETURN J. MEIGS, JR., Ohio.	1814.

ATTORNEYS-GENERAL.
CÆSAR A. RODNEY, Delaware.	1809.
WILLIAM PINCKNEY, Maryland.	1811.
RICHARD RUSH, Pennsylvania.	1814.

FINANCIAL CONDITION OF THE COUNTRY.

Year.	Imports.	Exports.	Expenditures.	Debt.
1809	$59,400,000	$52,203,333	$13,867,226	$57,023,192
1810	85,406,000	66,657,970	13,319,986	53,178,217
1811	53,100,000	61,316,883	13,601,808	48,005,587
1812	77,030,000	38,527,236	22,279,121	45,209,737
1813	22,005,000	27,855,927	39,190,520	55,962,827
1814	12,965,000	6,927,441	38,028,230	81,487,846
1815	113,041,274	52,557,753	39,582,493	99,833,660
1816	147,103,000	81,920,452	48,244,495	127,334,938

JAMES MADISON.

BIOGRAPHICAL SKETCH.

The fourth President of the United States, was James Madison, who was born in Orange County, Virginia, on the 16th of March, 1751. He was of Welsh descent, and his father James Madison, was among the early emigrants to Virginia.

He received a liberal education, and graduated at Princeton College, in 1771. He commenced the practice of law, but was called in early life, to attend to the public affairs of his State, and Country. In 1779 he was chosen a delegate to the conti-

JAMES MADISON.

nental Congress, and continued as such, until 1784. He was a delegate to the Convention, held at Philadelphia, in May, 1787, to frame the Constitution, and was one of its most distinguished members. He was also elected to the new Congress held at New York, in 1789.

In the year 1794, being then in his forty-third year, he married Mrs. Dolly Paine Todd, of Philadelphia, a widow lady much admired, and who was twenty-three years younger than Mr. Madison.

In his political views, Mr. Madison was a Democrat (then called Republican) and co-operated with Jefferson in his views of national policy. He was Secretary of State during Jefferson's administration, and in 1809, having received the nomination and support of the Democratic, or Anti Federal party, he succeeded Mr. Jefferson as President. The war of 1812, was declared during his administration against Great Britain, and the same year he was re-elected to the presidency. It was also during his administration, that the city of Washington was captured by the British, and the public buildings destroyed. Peace was also concluded at Ghent in 1814, which he sincerely desired.

He retired in 1817, to his residence at Montpelier, in Orange County, Virginia, being then sixty-six years of age. Subsequently, he was chosen a member of the State Convention, to revise the Constitution of his State, and for several years acted as Rector of the University of Virginia. At the age of eighty-five the earthly career of Mr. Madison was closed. He died respected and beloved, on the 28th of June, 1836.

MONROE'S ADMINISTRATION,

WITH

BIOGRAPHICAL SKETCH.
1817–1825.

TWO TERMS—EIGHT YEARS.

ELECTED BY THE REPUBLICANS [ANTI-FEDERALISTS.]

CABINET.

PRESIDENT:
James Monroe, Virginia.

VICE-PRESIDENT:
Daniel D. Tompkins, New York.

SECRETARY OF STATE:
John Quincy Adams, Massachusetts.

SECRETARY OF THE TREASURY.
William H. Crawford, Georgia.

SECRETARIES OF WAR:
Isaac Shelby, Kentucky. 1817.
John C. Calhoun, South Carolina. 1817.

SECRETARIES OF THE NAVY:
Benjamin W. Crowninshield, Mass. 1818.
Smith Thompson, New York. 1818.
Samuel L. Southard, New Jersey. 1823.

POSTMASTERS-GENERAL.
Return J. Meigs, Jr., Ohio. 1817.
John McLean, Ohio. 1823.

ATTORNEY-GENERAL.
William Wirt, Virginia.

FINANCIAL CONDITION OF THE COUNTRY.

Year.	Imports.	Exports.	Expenditures.	Debt.
1817	$99,250,000	$87,671,560	$40,877,616	$123,491,965
1818	121,750,000	93,281,133	35,164,875	103,466,633
1819	87,125,000	70,141,501	24,004,199	95,529,648
1820	74,150,000	69,661,669	21,763,024	91,015,566
1821	62,595,724	64,974,382	19,090,572	89,987,427
1822	83,241,541	72,160,281	17,676,592	93,546,676
1823	77,579,267	74,699,030	15,314,171	90,875,877
1824	89,549,007	75,986,657	31,898,538	90,269,777

JAMES MONROE.

BIOGRAPHICAL SKETCH.

James Monroe, the fifth President of the United States, was born on the 2d of April, 1759, in the county of Westmoreland, Virginia.

His parents, Spencer Monroe and Elizabeth Jones, descended from the first families of that State. He entered the college of William and Mary, but left his collegiate studies before he had graduated, for the purpose of joining the Standard of his Country, which he did in his eighteenth year, and hastened to

JAMES MONROE.

join Washington at his head-quarters, in the city of New York.

He was in many conflicts in the campaign of 1776, and was severely wounded in the battle of Trenton. During the campaigns of 1777, and 1778, he acted as aid to Lord Stirling, and distinguished himself in many battles, displaying great courage and coolness on the bloody fields of Brandywine, Germantown, and Monmouth. He subsequently studied law under Mr. Jefferson, while the latter was Governor of Virginia. In his twenty-fourth year, he was elected to the Legislature of his State, and in the following year, was elected a delegate to the Continental Congress, and thereafter represented his State in Congress, until 1876.

While in New York attending the Continental Congress, he married Miss Kortright, a beautiful and accomplished lady, daughter of Mr. L. Kortright of that city. Mr. Madison was opposed to the adoption of the Federal Constitution as framed by the Convention of 1787, and strongly urged that certain amendments should be made previous to its adoption.

In 1790, he was chosen, and took his place in the Senate of the United States, and continued therein for four years, acting with the Anti-Federal party in opposition to Washington's administration, notwithstanding which, Gen. Washington appointed him Minister to France in 1794, and subsequently, succeeded Mr. King as Minister to England.

In 1799, Mr. Monroe was elected Governor of Virginia, which office he filled for three years. Under the administrations both of Jefferson and Madison, he was appointed to many offices, and superintended many of the important matters and negotiations of the Government, thereby rendering essential, and invaluable services.

In 1816, Mr. Monroe was nominated for the Presidency by the Anti-Federal or Democratic party, and was elected to succeed Mr. Madison. His administration was exceedingly popular, and in 1820, he was almost unanimously re-elected, having received—excepting one—every vote of the Electoral Colleges. His first inauguration took place on the 4th of March, 1817, and his second, on Monday, the fifth of March, 1821. He died at the residence of his son-in-law, Samuel L. Gouveneur in the city of New York, on July 4th, 1831, being the fifty-fifth anniversary of our national independence.

J. Q. ADAMS'S ADMINISTRATION,

WITH

BIOGRAPHICAL SKETCH.
1825–1829.

ONE TERM—FOUR YEARS.

ELECTED BY THE REPUBLICAN PARTY.

CABINET.

PRESIDENT:
John Quincy Adams, Massachusetts.

VICE-PRESIDENT:
John C. Calhoun, South Carolina.

SECRETARY OF STATE:
Henry Clay, Kentucky.

SECRETARY OF THE TREASURY:
Richard Rush, Pennsylvania.

SECRETARIES OF WAR:
James Barbour, Virginia.   1825.
Peter B. Porter, New York. 1828.

SECRETARY OF THE NAVY:
Samuel L. Southard, New Jersey.

POST MASTER-GENERAL:
John McLean, Ohio.

ATTORNEY-GENERAL:
William Wirt, Virginia,

FINANCIAL CONDITION OF THE COUNTRY.

Year	Imports	Exports	Expenditures	Debt
1825	$96,340,075	$99,535,388	$23,585,804	$83,788,432
1826	84,974,477	77,595,322	24,103,398	81,054,059
1827	79,484,068	82,324,727	22,656,764	73,987,357
1828	88,509,824	72,264,686	25,459,479	67,475,043

JOHN QUINCY ADAMS.

BIOGRAPHICAL SKETCH.

The sixth President of the United States, was John Quincy Adams. He was the son of John Adams, the second President, and was born in his father's mansion, in the city of Boston, although the family seat was in the present town of Quincy, Massachusetts, on the 11th day of July 1767.

At the age of eleven years, he embarked for France with his father and remained there several months. He subsequently visited Holland, and in 1781, went with Mr. Dana (who had

JOHN QUINCY ADAMS.

been appointed minister) to Russia as his private secretary and remained there eighteen months. From 1783, to 1785, he was with his father in England, Holland, and France. He returned to the United States in 1785, entered Harvard College, and graduated in 1787. He then commenced the study of law at Newburyport under Mr. Theophilus Parsons, and after completing his studies, commenced the practice of his profession in Boston, devoting his leisure time in writing and publishing a series of tracts, and other papers, on the great political questions of the day.

In 1794, General Washington appointed him Minister Resident to the Netherlands, where he remained for two years. He was afterwards appointed Minister Plenipotentiary to Portugal, but on his way there, received an appointment transferring him to Lisbon, where he remained till 1801.

Mr. Adams was a moderate Federalist, and in 1803, was elected a Senator of the United States but not by a party vote. He supported Mr. Jefferson in such measures as his judgment approved. He was appointed one of the commissioners, by whom the treaty of peace was negotiated, between Great Britain and the United States at Ghent, in 1814. In 1815, he was appointed by Mr. Madison, Minister to Great Britain, where he remained about two years, he was then recalled by Mr. Monroe, and appointed by him, Secretary of State, which office he filled for eight years.

The canditates put in nomination to succeed Mr. Monroe, were General Jackson, Henry Clay, William H. Crawford and Mr. Adams. No choice was effected by the Electoral Colleges, by reason of there being so many in nomination, but General Jackson received the greatest number of votes. The election was thereupon referred to the House of Representatives, and on the first ballot, Mr. Adams received the vote of thirteen States and was elected. His inauguration took place on the 4th of March, 1825. John C. Calhoun was made Vice-President.

In May 1797, Mr. Adams was married to Louisa Catherine Johnson, daughter of Joshua Johnson of Maryland, who then resided in London. By this lady, he had four children, of whom, only one, Mr. Charles F. Adams of Boston, is now living.

On the twenty-second of Februry, 1848, this most accomplished scholar and statesman was prostrated by paralysis, while in his seat in the House of Representatives, and breathed his last on the following day. He died in the Speaker's room, in the Capitol, being in his eighty-first year. His dying words were " This is the last of earth."

JACKSON'S ADMINISTRATION,

WITH

BIOGRAPHICAL SKETCH.
1829–1837.

TWO TERMS—EIGHT YEARS.

ELECTED BY THE DEMOCRATIC PARTY.

CABINET.

PRESIDENT:
Andrew Jackson, Tennessee.

VICE PRESIDENTS:
John C. Calhoun, South Carolina.
Martin Van Buren, New York.

SECRETARIES OF STATE:
Martin Van Buren, New York.	1829.
Edward Livingston, Louisiana.	1831.
Lewis McLane, Delaware.	1833.
John Forsyth, Georgia.	1834.

SECRETARIES OF THE TREASURY:
Samuel D. Ingham, Pennsylvania.	1829.
Louis McLane, Delaware.	1831.
William J. Duane, Pennsylvania.	1833.
Roger B. Taney, Maryland.	1833.
Levi Woodbury, New Hampshire.	1834.

SECRETARIES OF WAR:
John H. Eaton, Tennessee.	1829.
Lewis Cass, Ohio.	1831.

SECRETARIES OF THE NAVY:
John Branch, North Carolina.	1829.
Levi Woodbury, New Hampshire.	1831.
Mahlon Dickerson, New Jersey.	1834.

POST MASTERS-GENERAL:
William T. Barry, Kentucky.	1829.
Amos Kendall, Kentucky.	1835.

ATTORNEYS-GENERAL:
John M. Berrien, Georgia.	1829.
Roger B. Taney, Maryland.	1831.
Benjamin F. Butler, New York.	1834.

FINANCIAL CONDITION OF THE COUNTRY.

Year.	Imports.	Exports.	Expenditures.	Debt.
1829	$74,492,527	$72,358,671	$25,044,358	$58,421,413
1830	70,876,920	73,849,508	24,585,281	48,565,406
1831	103,191,124	81,310,583	30,038,416	39,124,191
1832	101,029,266	87,176,943	34,356,698	24,322,235
1833	108,118,311	90,140,443	24,257,298	7,001,032
1834	126,521,332	104,336,973	24,601,982	4,760,081
1835	149,895,742	121,693,577	27,573,141	351,289
1836	189,980,085	128,663,040	30,934,664	291,089

ANDREW JACKSON.

BIOGRAPHICAL SKETCH.

Andrew Jackson, the seventh President of the United States, was of Scottish descent. His grandfather, Hugh Jackson, removed to Ireland, where his sons became respectable farmers. In 1765, his youngest son emigrated to North America, and settled in South Carolina, where he purchased a plantation at Waxhaw Settlement. On this plantation, Andrew Jackson was born on the 15th of March, 1767.

His father died about the time of his birth, leaving his

ANDREW JACKSON.

mother, whose maiden name was Elizabeth Hutchinson, a widow with three sons.

In the spring of 1779, South Carolina was invaded by the English, and his brother, Hugh Jackson, who had enlisted with others to repel them, lost his life in the fatigues of the service. At the age of thirteen, Andrew, with his brother

Robert, joined a company of volunteers and were engaged in a battle at a place called Hanging Rock, where the volunteers particularly distinguished themselves. Both of the young men were soon after taken prisoners, and as such, upon one occasion Andrew was ordered by a British officer to clean his boots, which he indignantly refused to do, whereupon, he was struck by the officer with his sword, causing a deep wound, the scar of which he carried with him to his grave.

His brother Robert, for refusing to perform like menial service, was treated in the same manner, and received a wound from which he never recovered. They were both finally exchanged, and Robert died two days after his arrival home. His mother going on board of a prison ship to nurse some sick, captive friends, took a fever from which she died soon after, leaving Andrew, then a young man, the sole survivor of the family.

When eighteen years of age, he commenced the study of law at Salisbury, North Carolina, and in due time was admitted to the bar, and commenced the practice of law in that State, but being appointed by the Governor, Solicitor for the Western District, which embraced Tennessee, he removed to Jonesborough in 1788, being then only twenty-one years of age. In this new and half-civilized region, he endured hardships and encountered dangers of every kind. His sensitive nature, strong passions, iron will, with his fearless and determined spirit, led him into many difficulties and personal quarrels, all of which he met manfully, ever ready to fight an enemy, or chastise an offender. His motto was, "Ask nothing but what is right; submit to nothing wrong."

On the admission of Tennessee into the Union, Jackson was chosen the first Representative to Congress, and took his seat in the House, on the 5th of December, 1796. His term there however, was short, for being elected by the Legislature, he took his seat in the Senate of the United States, on the 22nd of November, 1797.

In his views he was a democrat, and acted with the Democratic party. After resigning his seat as a Senator, he was appointed Judge of the Supreme Court of Tennessee, which office he held for six years and then resigned. In 1802, he was appointed Major General of the militia of the State. During the war of 1812, he took an active part in the campaigns against the Indians and British, in the capacity of Major General, and on the 23rd of December, 1814, obtained a great victory over them at New Orleans, and was hailed by the people of the South-West as their deliverer.

In 1828, he was nominated for the Presidency, by the Democratic party, the opposing candidate being John Quincy Adams. It was a most exciting campaign, but Jackson was elected, and again re-elected in 1832. His first inauguration took place on the 4th of March, 1829; his second, on the 4th of March, 1833. During his administration, many grave and important questions were agitated, which caused great excitement throughout the country; among these were those relating to the Tariff, U. S. Bank, Public Lands, nullification, Internal Improvement, etc., etc.

On the 3rd of March, 1837, he published his farewell address full of patriotism, good advice, and love of country. He then retired to the Hermitage in Tennessee, where he passed the remainder of his days, breathing his last on the 8th of June, 1845.

VAN BUREN'S ADMINISTRATION,

WITH

BIOGRAPHICAL SKETCH.
1837–1841.

ONE TERM—FOUR YEARS.

ELECTED BY THE DEMOCRATIC PARTY.

CABINET.

PRESIDENT:
Martin Van Buren, New York.

VICE-PRESIDENT:
Richard M. Johnson, Kentucky.

SECRETARY OF STATE:
John Forsyth, Georgia.

SECRETARY OF THE TREASURY:
Levi Woodbury, New Hampshire.

SECRETARY OF WAR:
Joel R. Poinsett, South Carolina.

SECRETARIES OF THE NAVY:
Mahlon Dickerson, New Jersey. 1837.
James K. Paulding, New York. 1841.

POST MASTERS-GENERAL:
Amos Kendall, Kentucky. 1837.
John M. Niles, Connecticut. 1840.

ATTORNEYS-GENERAL.
Benjamin F. Butler, New York. 1837.
Felix Grundy, Tennessee. 1838.
Henry D. Gilpin, Pennsylvania. 1840.

FINANCIAL CONDITION OF THE COUNTRY.

Year	Imports	Exports	Expenditures	Debt
1837	$140,989,217	$117,419,376	$37,265,037	$1,878,223
1838	113,717,401	108,486,616	39,455,439	4,857,600
1839	162,092,132	121,088,416	37,614,936	11,983,737
1840	107,641,519	132,085,936	28,226,553	5,125,077

MARTIN VAN BUREN.

BIOGRAPHICAL SKETCH.

The ancestors of Martin Van Buren, the eighth President of the United States, were among the early emigrants from Holland to the colony of New Netherlands, now the State of New York. His father, Abraham Van Buren, was a farmer in moderate circumstances. Martin, was born at Kinderhook, December 5th, 1782.

MARTIN VAN BUREN.

At the age of fourteen, he commenced the study of law in the office of Francis Sylvester, and completed his studies in the office of William P. Van Ness of New York city. He possessed an active, observing mind, attended all the meetings of the Democratic party, and gave much attention to the political subjects of the day.

In the twenty-first year of his age, he was admitted to the bar, as an Attorney at Law, and commenced its practice in his native village. He soon became one of the most distinguished members of his profession. In 1808, he was appointed Surrogate of Columbia County; in 1815, he was appointed Attorney. General of the State; in 1821, he was elected a Senator of the United States, by the Legislature of New York, and in 1828, was elected Governor of that State.

President Jackson having appointed him Secretary of State of the United States, he resigned his office as Governor on the 12th of March, 1829. Having retired from this office in June, 1831, he was appointed by the President, Minister to Great Britain, and arrived in London in September of that year. In May, 1832, he was nominated by the Democratic party as Vice-President, and was elected to that office. He was nominated as the successor of General Jackson by the same party, and received 170 votes of the Electoral College, against 124 for all other candidates. His inauguration took place the 4th of March, 1837.

At this time, the business of the Country was on the verge of prostration and ruin. Previous to this, their having been large facilities for obtaining bank loans, importation of foreign goods had immensely increased, and the spirit of speculation, especially in real estate, had assumed in 1836, the features of a mania. The money thus used in speculation, had been obtained from the Deposit Banks of the United States funds, but in 1836, Congress had authorized the Secretary of the Treasury, to distribute all the public funds, excepting $5,000,000, among the several States. This money after January, 1837, was accordingly taken from the Deposit Banks, thus compelling them to curtail their loans, which resulted in a serious pecuniary embarrassment.

Over trading, and speculation were therefore suddenly checked, and in the spring of 1837, heavy, and innumerable, mercantile failures took place in all our cities, and many banks suspended specie payment. The President recommended to Congress the measure known as the *Sub treasury scheme*, which subsequently passed. Mr. Van Buren was renominated for the Presidency but received only 60 votes of the Electoral College, against 234 for Harrison. He died on the 24th of July, 1862.

HARRISON'S AND TYLER'S ADMINISTRATIONS,

WITH

BIOGRAPHICAL SKETCHES.
1841–1845.

ONE TERM—FOUR YEARS.

ELECTED BY THE WHIGS.

President Harrison died April 4, 1841.

CABINET.

PRESIDENTS:
WILLLAM HENRY HARRISON, Ohio. 1841.
JOHN TYLER, Virginia. 1841.

VICE-PRESIDENT:
JOHN TYLER, Virginia. 1841

SECRETARIES OF STATE:
DANIEL WEBSTER, Massachusetts. 1841.
HUGH S. LEGARE, South Carolina. 1843.
ABEL P. UPSHUR, Virginia. 1843.
JOHN NELSON, Maryland. 1844.
JOHN C. CALHOUN, South Carolina. 1845.

SECRETARIES OF THE TREASURY.
THOMAS EWING, Ohio. 1841.
WALTER FORWARD, Pennsylvania. 1841.
JOHN C. SPENCER, New York. 1843.
GEORGE M. BIBB, KENTUCKY. 1844.

SECRETARIES OF WAR:
JOHN BELL, Tennessee. 1841.
JOHN C. SPENCER, New York, 1841.
JAMES M. PORTER, Pennsylvania. 1843.
WILLIAM WILKINS, Pennsylvania. 1844.

SECRETARIES OF THE NAVY:
GEORGE E. BADGER, N. Carolina. 1841.
ABEL P. UPSHUR, Virginia. 1841.
DAVID HENSHAW, Massachusetts, 1843.
THOMAS W. GILMER, Virginia. 1844.
JOHN Y. MASON, Virginia. 1844.

POSTMASTERS-GENERAL.
FRANCIS GRANGER, New York. 1841.
CHARLES A. WICKLIFFE, Kentucky. 1841.

ATTORNEYS-GENERAL.
JOHN J. CRITTENDEN, Kentucky. 1841.
HUGH S. LEGARE, South Carolina. 1841.
JOHN NELSON, Maryland. 1844.

NANCIAL CONDITION OF THE COUNTRY.

Year.	Exports.	Imports.	Expenditures.	Debt.
1841	$127,946,117	$121,851,803	$31,797,530	$6,737,398
1842	100,152,087	104,691,531	32,936,876	15,028,486
1843	64,753,799	84,346,480	12,118,105	27,203,450
1844	108,435,035	111,200,046	33,642,010	24,748,188

WILLIAM H. HARRISON.

BIOGRAPHICAL SKETCH.

William Henry Harrison, the ninth President of the United States, was the youngest son of Benjamin Harrison, one of the Signers of the Declaration of Independence, and one of the Governors of Virginia. William Henry, was born on the ninth of February, 1773, at Berkeley on the James River, Virginia.

He was educated at Hampden, Sydney College, Va., and applied himself to the study of medicine as a profession, but

WILLIAM H. HARRISON.

before its completion, he gave up his studies, and joined the army raised for the defence of the Ohio frontier against the Indians. He received his commission of Ensign in a regiment of artillery, from Gen. Washington, in 1791, and in 1792, was promoted to the rank of Lieutenant.

He soon after joined the new army under the command of

General Anthony Wayne at Pittsburgh, and remained with him some years, engaged in many battles with the Indians, at, and about Fort Washington, where Cincinnati now stands. After the campaign, which resulted in a treaty of peace with the Indians, he was promoted to the rank of Captain, and soon after, at the age of twenty-one, he married the daughter of John Cleves Symmes, the founder of the Miami Settlements.

In 1797, he was appointed by President Adams, Secretary, and *Ex Officio*, Lieutenant-Governor of the North Western Territory. In 1799, he was elected by the legislature of that territory, their first delegate to Congress at the age of twenty-six. Subsequently, the new territory of Indiana was established, which included what are now the States of Indiana, Illinois, Michigan, and Wisconsin, over which he was appointed Governor, and also Superintendent of Indian affairs, and Commander-in-chief of the militia.

He held the office of Governor for a period of thirteen years, having been successively appointed by Adams, Jefferson, and Madison, at the earnest solicitation of the people of the territory. He concluded many treaties with the Indians, and at one time obtained from them the cession of over 50,000,000 of acres, lying between the river Illinois and the Mississippi.

In 1811, he fought the memorable and desperate battle of Tippecanoe, and was very active in the war of 1812. In 1816, he was elected to represent the Congressional District of Ohio, in the House of Representatives of the United States, and subsequently held many other offices. In 1839, he was nominated for the Presidency, by the National Convention of Whig delegates, who had assembled at Harrisburgh, and was elected by an overwhelming majority. He received 234 Electoral votes against 60 for Mr. Van Buren.

The inauguration of General Harrison took place on the 4th of March, 1841, but his administration, however, was very brief. On the 27th of March, he was seized with a severe illness, which terminated his life on Sunday morning the 4th of April, just one month after his inauguration, in the sixty-eighth year of his age.

JOHN TYLER.

BIOGRAPHICAL SKETCH.

John Tyler, the tenth President of the United States, was born in Charles City County, Virginia, on the 29th of March, 1790. His ancestors were among the early English settlers of the Old Dominion. His father was one of the patriots of the Revolution, and devoted himself to its success.

At a very early age, Young Tyler was very much attached to his studies, and was so precocious, that he entered William and Mary College at the age of twelve years, and graduated

JOHN TYLER.

when he was but seventeen. He commenced the study of law, and at nineteen years of age, was admitted to the bar, no objection having been raised as to his age.

In 1811, he was elected a member of the House of Delegates, and took his seat in the Virginia Legislature, where he remained several years, and until 1816, when he was elected to Congress, then being but twenty-six years of age, and was twice re-elected, but by reason of ill health, was finally obliged to resign, and returned to the practice of his profession.

Mr Tyler was elected Governor of Virginia, in December, 1825, and during his administration, he urged forward, and greatly encouraged internal improvements, and many of the finest works in the State, were commenced, and completed, through his instrumentality. He was subsequently re-elected Governor, but before his term of office had expired, he was elected a Senator, having defeated John Randolph.

On the accession of Gen'l Jackson to the Presidency, Mr. Tyler supported his administration in many particulars, but yet, at times, took an independent course. With the nullifiers of South Carolina, he also sympathised; and when the President took his position against the anti-tariff and nullifying proceedings of that State, he withdrew his support from the Administration, acting with Mr. Calhoun, and contending for State Rights.

In 1839, he was elected one of the delegates from Virginia, to the Whig National Convention, at Harrisburg, and exerted his influence in favor of the nomination of Henry Clay, who was defeated by General Harrison, the nominee. It was deemed necessary by the Convention, after the nomination of Harrison, that the candidate for the Vice-President should be a Southern man, and without much reflection, it was offered to Mr. Tyler, who accepted.

On the 6th of April, 1841, after the death of General Harrison, Mr. Tyler took, and subscribed an oath of office, and then issued an inaugural address, to the people of the United States. He took such a course, however, that he lost the confidence of the party who nominated him, without gaining that of his political opponents, and in the late great rebellion, he took part with the enemies of the Republic.

In 1813, at the age of twenty-three, Mr. Tyler married Miss Letitia Christian, a lady much esteemed, and a member of the Episcopal Church. She died at Washington, in 1842. While President of the United States, he was again married to Miss Julia Gardiner, daughter of David Gardiner of New York. He died in Richmond, Virginia, on the 18th of January, 1862.

POLK'S ADMINISTRATION,

WITH

BIOGRAPHICAL SKETCH.
1845–1849.

ONE TERM—FOUR YEARS.

ELECTED BY THE DEMOCRATIC PARTY.

CABINET.

PRESIDENT:
JAMES K. POLK, Tennessee.

VICE PRESIDENT:
GEORGE M. DALLAS, Pennsylvania.

SECRETARY OF STATE:
JAMES BUCHANAN, Pennsylvania.

SECRETARY OF THE TREASURY:
ROBERT J. WALKER, Mississippi.

SECRETARY OF WAR:
WILLIAM L. MARCY, New York.

SECRETARIES OF THE NAVY:
GEORGE BANCROFT, Massachusetts. 1845.
JOHN Y. MASON, Virginia.   1846.

POST MASTER-GENERAL:
CAVE JOHNSON, Tennessee.

ATTORNEYS-GENERAL:
JOHN Y. MASON, Virginia.   1845.
NATHAN CLIFFORD, Maine.   1846.
ISAAC TOUCEY, Connecticut. 1848.

FINANCIAL CONDITION OF THE COUNTRY.

Year.	Imports.	Exports.	Expenditures.	Debt.
1845	$117,254,564	$114,646,606	$30,490,408	$17,093,794
1846	121,691,797	113,488,516	27,632,282	16,750,926
1847	146,545,638	158,618,622	60,520,851	38,926,623
1848	154,998,928	154,032,131	60,655,143	48,526,879

JAMES K. POLK.

BIOGRAPHICAL SKETCH.

James Knox Polk, the eleventh President of the United States, was born on the 2nd of November, 1795, in Mecklenburg County, North Carolina. His ancestors were emigrants from Ireland, who settled in Somerset County, on the eastern shore of Maryland.

His father was a plain farmer, but an energetic, enterprising man, a strong Democrat, and an ardent admirer and supporter of Jefferson. In 1806, he removed with his family to

JAMES K. POLK.

Tennessee. Having prepared himself, under Mr. Black, a classical teacher, his son James K. Polk, in 1815, entered the University of North Carolina, being then in his twentieth year, and in 1818, graduated with the highest honors of his class.

Having returned to Tennessee, he commenced the study of law in the office of Felix Grundy, was admitted to the bar at the close of 1820, and soon became a leading practitioner. In 1823, he was elected to the legislature of his State, and after two years, was elected to represent his District in Congress. He was a staunch Democrat, the personal and political friend of General Jackson, and a firm opponent of Mr. Adams.

He was elected Speaker of the House in 1835, and re-elected to that position in 1837. For fourteen years, he served his District in Congress; then declined a re-election, but subsequently, in 1839, was nominated for Governor, and was elected by a large majority. After serving two years, he was renominated, but was defeated by James C. Jones, the Whig candidate.

On the 29th of May, 1844, Mr. Polk received the nomination of the Democratic National Convention assembled at Baltimore, for President of the United States, and was subsequently elected, receiving 170 Electoral votes, against 105 for Henry Clay. George M. Dallas was elected Vice-President, by the same majority over Mr. Frelinghuysen.

He was inaugurated on the 4th of March, 1845. During his administration, war was commenced with Mexico, which resulted in a treaty, whereby California and New Mexico were ceded to the United States. The controversy with Great Britain, respecting the North West boundary, was also settled by treaty, and an independent treasury system was established.

After the inauguration of General Taylor, he returned to Tennessee where he expected to spend the remainder of his days in retirement; but his days were few. He was seized with the chronic diarrhoea about three months after his term of office had expired, and he died on the 15th of June, 1849, in the fifty-fourth year of his age.

TAYLOR'S AND FILLMORE'S ADMINISTRATIONS,

WITH

BIOGRAPHICAL SKETCHES.
1849–1853.

ONE TERM—FOUR YEARS.

ELECTED BY THE WHIGS.

President Taylor died July 9, 1850.

CABINET.

PRESIDENTS:
ZACHARY TAYLOR, Louisiana.   1849.
MILLARD FILLMORE, New York.   1850.

VICE-PRESIDENT:
MILLARD FILLMORE, New York.   1849.

SECRETARIES OF STATE:
JOHN M. CLAYTON, Delaware.   1849.
DANIEL WEBSTER, Massachusetts.   1850.
EDWARD EVERETT, Massachusetts.   1852.

SECRETARIES OF THE TREASURY.
WILLIAM M. MEREDITH, Penn.   1849.
THOMAS CORWIN, Ohio.   1850.

SECRETARIES OF WAR:
GEORGE W. CRAWFORD, Georgia.   1849.
CHARLES M. CONRAD, Louisiana.   1850.

SECRETARIES OF THE NAVY:
WILLIAM B. PRESTON, Virginia.   1849.
WM. A. GRAHAM, North Carolina.   1850.
JOHN P. KENNEDY, Maryland.   1852,

SECRETARIES OF THE INTERIOR.
THOMAS EWING, Ohio.   1849.
ALEX. H. H. STUART, Virginia.   1850.

POSTMASTERS-GENERAL.
JACOB COLLAMER, Vermont.   1849.
NATHAN K. HALL, New York.   1850.
SAMUEL D. HUBBARD, Connecticut.   1852.

ATTORNEYS-GENERAL.
REVERDY JOHNSON, Maryland.   1849.
JOHN J. CRITTENDEN, Kentucky.   1850.

FINANCIAL CONDITION OF THE COUNTRY.

Year.	Imports.	Exports.	Expenditures.	Debt.
1849	$147,857,439	$145,755,820	$56,886,422	$64,704,693
1850	178,138,318	151,898,790	44,604,718	64,228,238
1851	216,224,932	218,388,011	48,476,104	62,560,395
1852	212,945,442	209,658,366	46,712,608	65,130,692

ZACHARY TAYLOR.

BIOGRAPHICAL SKETCH.

Zachary Taylor, the twelfth President of the United States, was born in Orange County, Virginia, on the twenty-fourth of November, 1784. His father, Richard Taylor, served with valor and zeal throughout the Revolutionary war. He held the commission of Colonel, was engaged in many battles, and rendered valuable aid to General Washington at Trenton.

The year following the birth of Zachary, Colonel Richard Taylor emigrated with his family to Kentucky, and settled

ZACHARY TAYLOR.

near Louisville. He was one of the framers of the Constitution of Kentucky, and was for many years a member of the Legislature of that State.

The early education of Zachary was necessarily limited. He assisted his father on the farm, until he was past twenty-one years of age. He received a commission as Lieutenant in the Seventh Regiment of United States Infantry, from President Jefferson, on the third of May, 1808.

In 1810, he was married to Miss Margaret Smith, a lady of Maryland. In 1812, he was placed in command of Fort Harrison, where he was attacked by a large number of Indians, and for his heroic defence of the fort, the President conferred upon him the rank of Major by brevet.

On the 20th of April, 1819, Major Taylor received the commission of a Lieutenant Colonel, and in 1832, was promoted by President Jackson to the rank of Colonel. He was engaged in the war against Black Hawk, and subsequently against the Seminole Indians in Florida, and had command of the United States troops in the desperate and bloody battle of Okeechobee, where he was again victorious.

For the distinguished services rendered in this battle, he received the thanks of the President in 1838, and was promoted to the rank of Brigadier-General by brevet soon after. In the war with Mexico, General Taylor displayed great military skill, sound judgment, and heroic bravery, as evinced in the memorable battles of Palo Alto, Resaca de la Palma, and Buena Vista.

His determined bravery, and brilliant achievements during the campaigns in Mexico, secured him the love and admiration of the people of the United States. He had taken no active part in politics, but was considered a Whig.

At the Whig National Convention, which met at Philadelphia on the 1st of June, 1848, he received the nomination for the presidency on the fourth ballot, having received 171 votes, against 35 for Clay, 60 for Scott, and 14 for Webster. At the election in November, he received 163 of the Electoral votes, against 127 for General Cass, the Democratic candidate.

His inauguration took place on Monday, the 5th of March, 1849, before a very large assemblage of people.

Early in July, 1850, he was seized with an alarming illness, which, assuming the form of a billious fever, soon terminated his life. He died in the city of Washington, on the 9th of July, 1850, in the 66th year of his age, having discharged the duties of President, one year, four months and four days.

MILLARD FILLMORE.

BIOGRAPHICAL SKETCH.

Millard Fillmore, the thirteenth President of the United States, was born at Summer Hill, in Cayuga County, New York, January, 7th, 1800.

His father, Nathaniel Fillmore, was a farmer, but lost his property by reason of some defect in the title. In 1819, he removed to Erie County, New York, and purchased a small farm which he cultivated with his own hands. His mother's

MILLARD FILLMORE.

name was Phebe Millard; she was a daughter of Dr. Abiathar Millard, and died in 1831.

The early education of Mr. Fillmore was extremely limited, and at a suitable age he was apprenticed to a wool-carder, but he improved every leisure moment in reading and cultivating his mind, having an insatiable thirst for knowledge. He remained four years as an apprentice, when he was advised by the late Judge Wood, of Cayuga County, whose acquaintance he had formed, to quit his trade and study law, and he very generously offered to give him a place in his office, and to advance money to defray his expenses.

Having accepted this offer, he entered Judge Wood's office and remained there for two years, partially supporting himself, however, by teaching three months in each year. In the fall of 1821, he removed to Erie County and entered a law office in Buffalo. In 1826, he was married to Abigail Powers, daughter of Rev. Lemuel Powers, a lady very highly esteemed for her many virtues.

In 1827, Mr. Fillmore was admitted as an attorney, and in 1829, as a Counselor of the Supreme Court of that State. He formed a copartnership with an elder member of the bar in Buffalo, and continued a successful practice in that city till 1847, when he removed to Albany, having been elected Comptroller. Previous to this, however, he had served for several years in the Legislature of that State, and had won the confidence of all other members.

He was elected to Congress in the fall of 1832, and continued for several years to represent his District. In 1844, he reluctantly accepted the Whig nomination for Governor of New York, but was defeated. In 1848, he was nominated by the Whigs, in the National Convention, for Vice-President, being put upon the ticket with General Taylor, and received the same number of Electoral votes. After he had entered upon his duties of Vice-President, he exhibited great wisdom and firmness, and as the presiding officer of the Senate, he exercised great courtesy, and ability.

On the 10th of July, 1850, after the decease of General Taylor, Mr. Fillmore took his oath of office as President. The old Cabinet having resigned, he selected a new Cabinet of eminent men, including Daniel Webster, as Secretary of State. It was a critical period in the history of the Country, as many difficult and exciting questions were under discussion, but his messages were calm, conciliatory, yet firm, and many vexed questions were settled during his administration.

Mr. Fillmore has ever enjoyed the confidence and well wishes of his Countrymen, who considered him honest, capable, and faithful to the Constitution.

PIERCE'S ADMINISTRATION,

WITH

BIOGRAPHICAL SKETCH.
1853–1857.

ONE TERM—FOUR YEARS.

ELECTED BY THE DEMOCRATIC PARTY.

CABINET.

PRESIDENT:
Franklin Pierce, New Hampshire.

VICE-PRESIDENT:
William R. King, Alabama.

SECRETARY OF STATE:
William L. Marcy, New York.

SECRETARY OF THE TREASURY:
James Guthrie, Kentucky.

SECRETARY OF WAR:
Jefferson Davis, Mississippi.

SECRETARY OF THE NAVY:
James C. Dobbin, North Carolina.

SECRETARY OF THE INTERIOR:
Robert McClennand, Michigan.

POSTMASTER-GENERAL:
James Campbell, Pennsylvania.

ATTORNEY-GENERAL:
Caleb Cushing, Massachusetts.

FINANCIAL CONDITION OF THE COUNTRY.

Year	Imports	Exports	Expenditures	Debt
1853	$267,978,647	$230,976,157	$54,577,061	$67,340,628
1854	304,562,381	278,241,064	75,473,119	47,242,206
1855	261,468,520	275,156,846	66,164,775	39,969,731
1856	314,639,943	326,964,908	72,726,341	30,963,900

FRANKLIN PIERCE.

BIOGRAPHICAL SKETCH.

Franklin Pierce is the son of General Benjamin Pierce, an officer in the old War of Independence, and was born at Hillsborough, New Hampshire, November 23rd, 1804, and was the fourteenth President of the United States.

In early life he received a liberal education, and at sixteen years of age, entered Bowdoin College, at Brunswick, Maine. He graduated in 1824, studied law, and was admitted to prac-

FRANKLIN PIERCE.

tice at the bar in 1827, and by degrees attained the highest rank in his profession.

He became an active politician, and a warm supporter of General Jackson in 1828. The following year he was elected to represent his District in the State Legislature, where he remained four years. In 1833, he was elected to Congress, and represented his constituents for four years in the House of

Representatives, and was then elected by the Legislature of his State, to a seat in the Senate of the United States.

In 1834, he married the daughter of Rev. Dr. Appleton, formerly President of Bowdoin College, and subsequently removed to Concord, which has since been his place of residence. When the war with Mexico broke out, he was active in raising the New England regiment of Volunteers, and having been commissioned a Brigadier-General, he joined the army in Mexico under General Scott, where he distinguished himself in many hard-fought battles.

At the Democratic Convention held in Baltimore, in 1852, he was unexpectedly nominated as the candidate for the next Presidency. He was elected by an overwhelming majority, having received 254 of the Electoral votes, while General Scott, the opposing candidate, received only 42. William R. King, of Alabama, was elected Vice-President, but was unable to take his seat by reason of increasing ill-health, which terminated his life in April, 1853.

Mr. Pierce was inaugurated as President on the 4th of March, 1853, and at the expiration of his term of office, he retired to private life, where he has since remained.

BUCHANAN'S ADMINISTRATION,

WITH

BIOGRAPHICAL SKETCH.
1857–1861.

ONE TERM—FOUR YEARS.

ELECTED BY THE DEMOCRATIC PARTY.

CABINET.

PRESIDENT:
JAMES BUCHANAN, Pennsylvania.
VICE-PRESIDENT:
JOHN C. BRECKINRIDGE, Kentucky.
SECRETARIES OF STATE:

LEWIS CASS, Michigan.	1857.
JEREMIAH S. BLACK, Pennsylvania.	1860.

SECRETARIES OF THE TREASURY:

HOWELL COBB, Georgia.	1857.
PHILIP F. THOMAS, Maryland.	1860.
JOHN A. DIX, New York.	1861.

SECRETARIES OF WAR:

JOHN B. FLOYD, Virginia.	1857.
JOSEPH HOLT, Kentucky.	1861.

SECRETARY OF THE NAVY:

ISAAC TOUCEY, Connecticut.	1857.

SECRETARY OF THE INTERIOR.

JACOB THOMPSON, Mississippi.	1857.

POST MASTERS-GENERAL:

AARON V. BROWN, Tennessee.	1857.
JOSEPH Holt, Kentucky.	1859.
HORATIO KING, Maine.	1861.

ATTORNEYS-GENERAL:

JEREMIAH S. BLACK, Pennsylvania.	1857.
EDWIN M. STANTON, Pennsylvania.	1860.

FINANCIAL CONDITION OF THE COUNTRY.

Year	Imports	Exports	Expenditures	Debt
1857	$362,890,141	$362,960,608	$71,274,587	$29,060,386
1858	282,613,150	324,614,421	82,002,186	44,910,777
1859	338,768,130	356,789,461	83,678,643	58,754,699
1860	362,162,541	400,122,296	77,055,125	64,769,703

JAMES BUCHANAN.

BIOGRAPHICAL SKETCH.

James Buchanan, the fifteenth President of the Republic, was of Irish parentage, and was born in Franklin County, Pennsylvania, on the 23rd of April, 1791. He received a liberal education, and graduated at Dickinson College with the highest honors, at the early age of eighteen years.

He studied law in the office of James Hopkins, of Lancaster, and in due time was admitted to the bar, and soon became

JAMES BUCHANAN.

a successful practitioner, attaining a high rank in his profession.

In 1814, when but twenty-three years of age, he was elected to the Legislature of his State, and in 1820, was sent to represent his District in Congress, where he remained for ten years, taking an active part in all of its proceedings and becoming distinguished as a debater.

He was a warm and consistent supporter of President Jackson, who appointed him a Minister to Russia in 1831. In 1834, he was elected to a seat in the United States Senate, and represented his constituents in that body for ten years.

In 1845, he was appointed Secretary of State, by President Polk, and acted as such during his term of service, and at the expiration thereof, retired to private life. In 1853, he was appointed Minister to England by President Pierce, in which official position he exhibited all the great qualities of an eminent Statesman.

Mr. Buchanan was nominated as a candidate for the Presidency, by the Democratic National Convention which assembled at Cincinnati, in June, 1856, and after a most exciting canvass he was elected by a large majority. The opposing candidates were Ex-President Fillmore, nominated by a National Convention of the American Party, and John C. Fremont, nominated by a National Convention of Republicans.

The last year of his term of office was an eventful one: the Slavery question had been revived, and the most intense excitement existed in the public mind. For months previously, a band of conspirators, including three or four members of his Cabinet, had been plotting treason against the government, and when in November, 1860, Abraham Lincoln was elected to the Presidency, this treason broke out into open rebellion, and in December, 1860, the first of the Southern States seceded, and others soon followed.

Mr. Buchanan, insisting that he had no right to coerce a State, even in rebellion, and possessed no Constitutional power to use the army and navy to put down the rebellion, passively sat, with closed eyes and folded arms; which inaction greatly encouraged the conspirators, to go on and complete their work of destroying the Nation.

After the close of his administration, he retired to Wheatland, near Lancaster, Pennsylvania, where he died, June 1st, 1868.

LINCOLN'S ADMINISTRATION,

WITH

BIOGRAPHICAL SKETCH.
1861–1865.

ELECTED BY THE REPUBLICAN PARTY FOR TWO TERMS.

Administered Four Years, One Month and Eleven Days.

Was assassinated the 14th of April 1865. Died April 15th, 1865.

CABINET.

PRESIDENT:
Abraham Lincoln, Illinois.

VICE-PRESIDENTS:
Hannibal Hamlin, Maine.
Andrew Johnson, Tennessee.

SECRETARY OF STATE:
William H. Seward, New York.

SECRETARIES OF THE TREASURY:
Salmon P. Chase, Ohio.	1861.
William Pitt Fessenden, Maine.	1864.
Hugh McCulloch, Indiana.	1865.

SECRETARIES OF WAR:
Simon Cameron, Pennsylvania.	1861.
Edwin M. Stanton, Pennsylvania.	1862.

SECRETARY OF THE NAVY:
Gideon Wells, Connecticut.	1861.

SECRETARIES OF THE INTERIOR.
Caleb B. Smith, Indiana.	1861.
John P. Usher, Indiana.	1863.

POSTMASTERS-GENERAL:
Montgomery Blair, Maryland.	1861.
William Dennison, Ohio.	1864.

ATTORNEYS-GENERAL:
Edward Bates, Missouri.	1861.
James J. Speed, Kentucky.	1864.

FINANCIAL CONDITION OF THE COUNTRY.

Year	Imports	Exports	Expenditures	Debt
1861	$286,598,135	$243,971,277	$85,387,313	$90,867,828
1862	275,357,051	229,938,985	570,841,700	514,211,371
1863	252,919,920	322,359,254	895,796,630	1,098,796,181
1864	329,562,895	301,984,561	1,298,144,656	1,740,690,489

LINCOLN'S INAUGURATION.

ABRAHAM LINCOLN.

BIOGRAPHICAL SKETCH.

Abraham Lincoln, the sixteenth President of the United States, was born in Hardin County, Kentucky, February 12th, 1809. His education in early life was quite limited. In 1816, his parents removed with him to Spencer County, Indiana, and subsequently he romoved to Illinois.

In 1830, he was a clerk in a store; in 1832, was a Captain of Volunteers in the Black Hawk war, and in 1834, was elected to the Legislature of the State of Illinois, where he served four years.

In 1836, he was licensed to practice law in the courts of that State, and he commenced his profession at Springfield, in 1837.

Mr. Lincoln soon rose to distinction, and became a prominent leader of the Whig party in Illinois. He canvassed the entire State for Henry Clay in 1844, and in 1846, was elected to Congress, where he served his constituents with fidelity.

On the 16th of May, 1860, the Representatives of the Republican party assembled in Convention, in an immense building called "The Wigwam," erected for that purpose in Chicago, and on the 19th, they nominated Mr. Lincoln as their candidate for the Presidency, and Hannibal Hamlin of Maine, for the Vice-Presidency. There were three other candidates for the Presidency in the field, viz; John Bell, nominated by the *Constitutional Union Party*; Stephen A. Douglass, by the regular *Democratic Convention*, and John C. Breckenridge, by the *Seceders* from that Convention, calling themselves the *National Democratic Convention*. Mr. Lincoln was elected, having received 180 of the Electoral votes, or 57 more than all his opponents.

He was inaugurated on the 4th of March, 1861, amid intense excitement. Violence was apprehended, but General Scott having made ample provision to preserve the peace, all passed off quietly. The rebellion having broken out into open hostilities, commencing with the seizure of Government property, and the attack on Fort Sumter, the President, on the 15th of April, 1861, issued his first call for seventy-five thousand men. On the 1st of January, 1863, he issued his Emancipation Proclamation, declaring all slaves in the rebellious States free.

In November, 1864, Mr. Lincoln, having again received the

MEDAL FROM THE FRENCH DEMOCRATS.

nomination was re-elected to the Presidency, with Andrew Johnson as Vice-President; they were inaugurated on the 4th of March, 1865, and the following month General Lee surrendered his army, thus virtually terminating the rebellion.

On the 2nd of April, the President, by proclamation, declared the war to be at an end.

There was great rejoicing throughout the Republic, in the great success of our arms, and the bright prospect of peace, soon, however, to be changed to grief and mourning. On the 14th of April, our lamented President was shot through the head by one John Wilkes Booth, while seated with his wife in a private box, in Ford's theatre in Washington, causing his death the following morning, he then being fifty-six years of age. It was the result of a conspiracy to assassinate, not only the President, but also members of his Cabinet and others. His remains were interred in the Oak Ridge Cemetery, at Springfield, Illinois.

*MEDAL FROM THE FRENCH DEMOCRATS.

*The above Engraving, represents a magnificent Gold Medal, which was presented by forty thousand French Democrats, to the President's widow, to express their sympathy for Our Republic, in the loss of so illustrious a Chief Magistrate. It is in outline, about one third less in size than the original—For a full description of it, see "Civil War in America," by Lossing.—

JOHNSON'S ADMINISTRATION,

WITH

BIOGRAPHICAL SKETCHES.
1865—1869.

AS VICE-PRESIDENT, HE SUCCEEDS MR. LINCOLN FOR

REMAINDER OF TERM.

CABINET.

PRESIDENT:
ANDREW JOHNSON, Tennessee.

SECRETARY OF STATE:
WILLIAM H. SEWARD, New York.

SECRETARY OF THE TREASURY:
HUGH McCULLOCH, Indiana.

SECRETARIES OF WAR:
EDWIN M. STANTON, Pennsylvania.	1865.
ULYSSES S. GRANT, Illinois.	1867.
EDWIN M. STANTON, Pennsylvania.	1868.
JOHN M. SCHOFIELD, Missouri.	1868.

SECRETARY OF THE NAVY:
GIDEON WELLS, Connecticut.	1865.

SECRETARIES OF THE INTERIOR.
JOHN P. USHER, Indiana.	1865.
JAMES HARLAN, Iowa.	1865.
ORVILLE, H. BROWNING, Illinois.	1866.

POST MASTERS-GENERAL:
WILLIAM DENNISON. Ohio.	1865.
ALEX. W. RANDALL, Wisconsin.	1866.

ATTORNEYS-GENERAL:
JAMES SPEED,	1865.
HENRY STANBERRY, Ohio.	1866.
WILLIAM M. EVARTS, New York.	1868.

FINANCIAL CONDITION OF THE COUNTRY.

Year	Imports	Exports	Expenditures	Debt
1865	$234,339,810	$336,697,123	$1,897,674,224	$2,682,593,026
1866	445,512,158	550,684,299	1,141,072,666	2,783,425,879
1867	411,733,309	438,577,312	1,093,079,655	2,692,199,215
1868	373,400,448	454,301,713	1,069,889,970	2,636,320,964

ANDREW JOHNSON.

BIOGRAPHICAL SKETCH.

Andrew Johnson, the seventeenth President of the United States, was born in Raleigh, North Carolina, on the 29th of December, 1808. At an early age he was apprenticed to learn the business of a tailor, and continued at the trade for several years.

Unlike most of the young men of this country, he grew up in

ANDREW JOHNSON.

utter ignorance of the most common branches of an English education, and was not able either to read or write until he was twenty years of age, after removing to Greenville in East Tennessee. He subsequently became an Alderman of that place, and in 1836, was elected Mayor, which office he filled for three years.

In 1835, he was chosen to the State Legislature, and in 1843, he was elected to Congress, and represented his State therein for several years. In 1853, he was chosen Governor of Tennessee, and was re-elected to that office.

In 1857, he was elected United States Senator, and was subsequently, in 1862, appointed by President Lincoln, Military Governor of Tennessee. He had previously been a Democrat in politics, and in the election of 1860, had used his influence to elect Mr. Breckenridge to the Presidency. He professed, however, to have changed his views materially, condemned the course of the South in the rebellion, and supported the measures of President Lincoln.

The Union National Convention, held at Baltimore, in June, 1864, nominated Mr. Lincoln for the Presidency, and Mr. Johnson for the Vice-Presidency, and in November, they were elected by a large majority.

On the 15th of April, 1865, a few hours after the death of Mr. Lincoln, he took the oath of office as President of the United States. Disagreements soon arose between Congress and the President, respecting the reconstruction of the States lately in rebellion, and it soon became evident that he was more friendly to the late enemies of the country, than he was to her true, and tried friends. He issued an order to Mr. Stanton, removing him from his office of Secretary of War, and performed many acts, considered by the majority of the people, as highly improper in a Chief Magistrate.

On the 22nd of February, 1868, by a vote of 126 to 47, it was resolved by the House of Representatives, that Andrew Johnson, President, be impeached of high crimes and misdemeanors. Articles of impeachment were prepared and presented, and on the 5th of March, 1868, the Senate of the United States, for the first time, was organized as a court for the trial of the President. Chief-Justice Salmon P. Chase presided. The trial continued from the 30th of March, to the 6th of May, 1868, when the case was submitted to the Senate. Its decision was given on the 26th of May. Thirty-five found him guilty, and nineteen voted "Not guilty."

In order to convict, it was necessary that two thirds should vote in the affirmative; one vote of the required number being wanted, he was acquitted.

GRANT'S ADMINISTRATION,

WITH

BIOGRAPHICAL SKETCH.
1869–1872.

ONE TERM—FOUR YEARS.

ELECTED BY THE REPUBLICAN PARTY.

CABINET.

PRESIDENT:
ULYSSES S. GRANT, Illinois.

VICE-PRESIDENT:
SCHUYLER COLFAX, Indiana.

SECRETARY OF STATE:
HAMILTON FISH, New York.

SECRETARY OF THE TREASURY.
GEORGE S. BOUTWELL, Massachusetts.

SECRETARIES OF WAR:
JOHN A. RAWLINS, Illinois.   1869.
WILLIAM W. BELKNAP, Iowa.   1869.

SECRETARIES OF THE NAVY:
ADOLPHE E. BORIE, Pennsylvania.   1869.
GEORGE M. ROBESON, New Jersey.   1869.

SECRETARIES OF THE INTERIOR.
JACOB D. COXE, Ohio.   1869.
COLUMBUS DELANO, Ohio.   1870.

POSTMASTER-GENERAL.
JOHN A. J. CRESWELL, Maryland.   1869.

ATTORNEYS-GENERAL.
E. ROCKWOOD HOAR, Massachusetts. 1869.
GEORGE H. WILLIAMS, Oregon.   1869.

STATEMENT OF THE PUBLIC DEBT.
JUNE 1, 1872.

Total amount of Principal,............................$2,260,290,351
"   "   "   Interest,..................................35,543,172

TOTAL DEBT,......................................$2,295,833,523

Cash in the Treasury, Coin,..........................$91,108,331
"   "   "   Currency,...............................11,207,813
                                         $102,316,144

DEBT LESS CASH IN TREASURY,..............................$2,193,517,378

DECREASE OF DEBT FROM MARCH 1ST., 1869 TO JUNE 1ST., 1872, $331,945,881

ULYSSES S. GRANT.

BIOGRAPHICAL SKETCH.

Our present chief magistrate, Ulysses S. Grant, being the eighteenth President of the United States, is of English descent. His grandfather, Noah Grant, was born in Coventry, Connecticut, on the 23d of June, 1748. He took an active part in the battle of Lexington, in the capacity of a Lieutenant, and

ULYSSES S. GRANT.

served through the Revolutionary war, having been promoted to the rank of Captain.

He subsequently removed to Westmoreland County, Penn., where, on the 23d of January, 1794, his father, Jesse Root Grant was born. In 1799, the family removed to Ohio, and on the 27th of April, 1822, at Point Pleasant, Clarmont County,

Ohio, in a small frame, one-story dwelling, was born Ulysses S. Grant, the subject of this sketch.

His mother's maiden name was Hannah Simpson; she was the only daughter of a thrifty farmer, a lady much beloved and respected.

A few months after his birth, his father removed to Georgetown, in Brown County, where he prosecuted successfully his business as a tanner. The early education of Ulysses was very much neglected, and being passionately fond of horses, most of his time was spent in driving the "team," and making himself useful to his father. He subsequently attended school at Maysville, Kentucky, and at the Academy at Ripley.

Through the influence of Thomas L. Hamer, a Member of Congress from the Georgetown district, he received an appointment to the Military Academy at West Point, and at once applied himself to study, under a professional teacher, and on the 15th of May, 1839, he started for West Point, being then in his eighteenth year.

He soon became initiated, and grew quite popular among the cadets, for his modesty and amiability, and was nicknamed "Uncle Sam." He was a fair scholar, but excelled in mathematics.

On the 30th of June, 1843, Grant graduated, being the twenty-first, on a list of thirty-nine. These were all that were left of more than one hundred who had entered the class with him. He was at once appointed brevet second Lieutenant in the Fourth Infantry, and took an active part in the Mexican War which followed, exhibiting at all times, great coolness and bravery, and at the close of which, he bore the brevet rank of Captain. In 1853, he was promoted to the rank of full Captain.

At St. Louis, on the 22nd of August, 1848, Grant married Miss Julia B. Dent, daughter of Colonel Frederick Dent, a young lady, very attractive in her manners, and amiable in disposition, whom he had known, and to whom he had been engaged for some years.

In 1854, he resigned his commission, and having lost some sixteen hundred dollars by the sutler of his regiment, he found himself reduced to poverty and want, against which he struggled for several years, without means, and without any legitimate business.

His father, Colonel Dent, had given his daughter Julia, sixty acres of land from his farm at Whitehaven, and also three or four slaves. On this land he built himself a small house, hauling the logs for its walls, and splitting the shingles for the roof with his own hands. This place he named "Hardscrabble," suggested by the hard struggle he experienced in obtaining from it sufficient for the bare sustenance of his family.

After four years of hard labor upon his small farm, and after expending some two thousand dollars his father had advanced him, he gave up farming as a failure, and went into partnership with one Mr. Boggs, at St. Louis, Mo., as real estate agents.

This copartnership commenced January 1st, 1859, and continued for about nine months, when, finding the business would not support two families, the copartnership was dissolved. From this time, to March, 1860, Captain Grant had no permanent business, although he had a wife and four children to support.

In March, 1860, he removed with his family to Galena, Illinois, his father and brothers having offered him a situation in their store, at an annual salary of six hundred dollars per annum, with the promise of an interest in the business, at some future time. His father had been successful in business, and was worth from seventy-five to one hundred thousand dollars at this time.

About the 1st of May, 1861, after the breaking out of the rebellion, through the influence of Elihu B. Washburne, and others, Governor Yates, of Illinois, took him into his office, as his military adviser, and Adjutant-General. He had previously to this, tendered his services to the Government at Washington, but his letter had been unanswered.

On the 4th of May, he was put in command of Camp Yates, during the absence of Captain Pope, and subsequently mustered several regiments into the service. On the 16th of June, he was appointed Colonel of the Twenty-First Illinois Volunteers, and requested to take command at once. Of his commission, Governor Yates subsequently said, "It was the most glorious day of my life when I signed it."

Being without horse, or uniform, he obtained the indorsement of an old friend to his note for three hundred dollars, which he got discounted, and with the proceeds, purchased them. His regiment was first ordered to Mexico, in Missouri, and there being no means of transportation, he marched them across the country on foot. In two months afterwards, Colonel Grant was appointed a Brigadier-General, his commission dating back to the 17th of May.

From this time, his promotion from rank to rank was rapid. In the battles in which he was engaged, he exhibited the same military qualities, as had been displayed by General Taylor in Mexico. Cool, calculating, persevering, and brave, he went into a fight expecting to be victorious, and when he was whipped, he did not "see it," and consequently did not "stay whipped."

In his first battle at Belmont, where he handled three thousand men so successfully, when a member of his staff, who had never been under fire before, rode up to him exclaiming, "Why, General, we are entirely lost! They have surrounded us!" he replied, apparently unmoved, "Well then, we will cut our way out. We have whipped them once to-day, and I think we can again."

His subsequent brilliant campaigns, did not secure him from the vilest of slanders. He was denounced as a drunkard, as being blood-thirsty, reckless of human life, incompetent, an utterly unfit to command a large body of troops. President Lincoln was strongly urged to remove him. After his capture of Vicksburg, however, where in the capitulation, he received fifteen Generals, about thirty-thousand soldiers, and one hundred and seventy-two cannon, President Lincoln sent him that remarkable autograph letter, dated July 16th, 1863, wherein, after acknowledging the great services, he had rendered the Country, he concludes with these words, "I now wish to make the personal acknowledgement, *that you were right, and I was wrong.*"

In 1864, a bill passed Congress, reviving the grade of Lieutenant-General, and authorizing the Executive to confer it upon some officer. This high rank in 1798, was created for Washington, in anticipation of a war with France. It was discontinued when he died. After the Mexican war, it was conferred by brevet on Winfield Scott. At the time of the passage of the bill, no other Americans had ever held it.

This bill, being passed, and Grant having been appointed to this office, by the President, he was telegraphed to report to the War Department in person, which he did, and received personally from the President, the commission. Soon after this he started West, and upon his arrival at Nashville, found an order from the War Department, formally assigning him to the command of *all the forces of the United States*, with headquarters in the field.

He made short work with the rebellion, and upon the surrender of Lee and his army, it was virtually at an end. General Grant's military career, from beginning to end, was a glorious one. He has fought more battles, and gained more victories, has captured more prisoners, and taken more guns than any General of modern times.

On the 12th of August, 1867, President Johnson suspended Stanton, and made Grant Secretary of War *ad interim*. The Senate subsequently refused to sanction this suspension, whereupon Grant surrendered the office to Stanton, against the wishes of President Johnson.

On the 20th of May, at a National Convention of the Republican party held in Chicago, General Grant was *unanimously* nominated for the Presidency, and Schuyler Colfax for the Vice-Presidency, both of whom were elected by large majorities over Seymour and Blair, the opposing candidates, and he was inaugurated on the 4th of March, 1869.

The administration of President Grant has been financially, a successful one. At the commencement of his term, March 4th, 1869, the aggregate debt of the Country was nearly two billions, six hundred and thirty millions of dollars. Since then it has rapidly decreased. On the 1st of December 1871, it had decreased *two hundred and seventy-seven millions.* The decrease from March 1st, 1869, to March 1st, 1872, was nearly three hundred millions and on the 1st of June, 1872, the decrease had amounted in the aggregate, to over three hundred and thirty millions since he went into office. We are at peace with foreign nations, and the Country is in a highly prosperous condition.

Notwithstanding all this, many are dissatisfied with his administration, and are opposed to his re-election; among these, is Senator Sumner, who very recently, in the Senate of the United States, made a most bitter and sarcastic speech personally denouncing him, the reason and justice of which, we leave it for the people to determine. He has since been renominated for the Presidency, an account of which, will be hereafter given.

ELECTORAL VOTES

FOR

President and Vice-President of the United States,

UNDER THE CONSTITUTION.

FIRST TERM—1789 TO 1793

At the time of this election, only eleven states had ratified the Constitution. North Carolina and Rhode Island had rejected it, and the Legislature of New York, by reason of some disagreement between the two branches, had failed in passing a law respecting the choosing of the Electors, and consequently no Electors were appointed to represent that State. Only *ten States*, therefore, participated in the election.

By the Constitution, as it then stood, the presidential electors voted for *two persons*, and the one receiving the highest number of votes, was to be the President, and the one having the next highest number, was to be the Vice-President. It was necessary that the President should receive a *majority* of the whole number of electoral votes, but this was not necessary to elect the Vice-President.

Whole number of Electors, 69.

ELECTORAL VOTE—George Washington, 69; John Adams, 34; John Jay, 9; R. H. Harrison, 6; John Rutledge, 6; John Hancock, 4; George Clinton, 3; Samuel Huntington, 2; John Milton, 2; James Armstrong, 1; Edward Telfair, 1; Benjamin Lincoln, 1.

George Washington was thereupon declared the President, and John Adams, the Vice-President.

SECOND TERM—1793 TO 1797.

Fifteen states participated in this election; Rhode Island and North Carolina having ratified the Constitution, and two new States, Vermont and Kentucky, having been admitted into the Union.

Whole number of Electors, 132.
ELECTORAL VOTE—George Washington, 132; John Adams, 77; George Clinton, 50; Thomas Jefferson, 4; Aaron Burr, 1.
George Washington was therefore again declared the President, and John Adams the Vice-President.

THIRD TERM—1797 TO 1801.

Tennessee having been admitted, the whole number of States, 16.
Whole number of Electors, 138.
ELECTORAL VOTE—John Adams, 71; Thomas Jefferson, 68; Aaron Burr, 30; Samuel Adams, 15; Oliver Ellsworth, 11; George Clinton, 7; John Jay, 5; James Iredell, 3; George Washington, 2; John Henry, 2; S. Johnson, 2; Charles C. Pinckney, 1.
John Adams was therefore declared the President, and Thomas Jefferson the Vice-President.

FOURTH TERM—1801 TO 1805.

Whole number of States, 16.
Whole number of Electors, 188.
ELECTORAL VOTE—Thomas Jefferson, 73; Aaron Burr, 73; John Adams, 65; Charles C. Pinckney, 64; John Jay, 1.
The votes for Jefferson and Burr being the highest, and *equal*, there was no election. It was necessary, therefore, under the Constitution, that the House of Representatives should decide which one was to be President, and which one Vice-President. On the 36th *ballot*, Mr. Jefferson was chosen President, and Mr. Burr Vice-President.

FIFTH TERM—1805 TO 1809.

Previous to this election, an amendment to the Constitution relative to the election of President and Vice-President had been proposed, *so as to designate which person had been voted for* as President, and which one as Vice-President. This Amendment had passed both branches of Congress, and in 1804, it had been ratified by the Legislatures of three-fourths of the States as required by the Constitution, and on the 25th of September, 1804, it was announced by the Secretary of State, as having been duly adopted and ratified. Hence at this election, they were voted for separately. Ohio had also been admitted into the Union.

Whole number of States, 17.
Whole number of Electors, 176.
ELECTORAL VOTE.—For President, Thomas Jefferson, 162; Charles C. Pinckney, 14.
For Vice-President, George Clinton, 162; Rufus King, 14.

Mr. Jefferson was therefore declared the President elect, and Mr. Clinton the Vice-President.

SIXTH TERM—1809 TO 1813.

Whole number of States, 17.
Whole number of Electors, 175.
ELECTORAL VOTE.—For President, James Madison, 122; George Clinton, 6; C. C. Pinckney, 47;
For Vice-President, George Clinton, 113; James Madison, 3; James Monroe, 3; John Langdon, 9,; Rufus King, 47;

Mr. Madison was therefore declared the President elect, and Mr. Clinton the Vice-President.

SEVENTH TERM—1813 TO 1817.

Whole number of States, 18.
Whole number of Electors, 217.
ELECTORAL VOTE.—For President, James Madison, 128; De Witt Clinton, of New York, 89.
For Vice-President, Elbridge Gerry, 131; Jared Ingersoll, 86.

Mr. Madison was therefore declared the President elect, and Mr. Gerry the Vice-President.

ELECTORAL VOTES. 187

EIGHTH TERM—1817 TO 1821.

Whole number of States, 19.
Whole number of Electors, 217.

ELECTORAL VOTE.— For President, James Monroe, 183; Rufus King, 34.

For Vice-President, Daniel D. Tompkins, 183; John E. Howard, 22; James Ross, 5; John Marshall, 4; Robert G. Harper, 3.

Mr. Monroe was therefore declared the President elect, and Daniel D. Tompkins, Vice-President.

NINTH TERM—1821 TO 1825.

Whole number of States, 24.
Whole number of Electors, 282.

ELECTORAL VOTE.—For President, James Monroe, 231; John Quincy Adams, 1.

For Vice-President, Daniel D. Tompkins, 218; Richard Stockton, 8; Robert G. Harper, 1; Richard Rush, 1; Daniel Rodney, 1.

Mr. Madison, was therefore declared the President elect, and Mr. Tompkins the Vice-President.

TENTH TERM—1825 TO 1829.

Whole number of States, 24.
Whole number of Electors, 261.

ELECTORAL VOTE.—For President, Andrew Jackson, 99; John Quincy Adams, 84; William H. Crawford, 41; Henry Clay, 37.

For Vice-President, John C. Calhoun, 182: Nathan Sanford, 30; Nathaniel Macon, 24; Andrew Jackson, 13; Martin Van Buren, 9; Henry Clay, 2.

Neither of the candidates for the Presidency receiving a *majority*, there was no election, and the vote was carried to the House of Representatives, where Adams received the vote of 13 States, Jackson of 7 States, and Crawford of 4 States.

Adams was therefore elected President, and John C. Calhoun, the Vice-President.

ELEVENTH TERM—1829 TO 1833.

Whole number of States, 24.
Whole number of Electors, 261.
ELECTORAL VOTE.—For President, Andrew Jackson, 178; John Quincy Adams, 83;
For Vice-President, John C. Calhoun, 171; Richard Rush, 83; William Smith, 7.
POPULAR VOTE.—For President, Jackson, 650,028; Adams, 512,158.
Mr. Jackson, was therefore declared the President elect, and Mr. Calhoun, the Vice-President.

TWELFTH TERM—1833 TO 1837.

Whole number of States, 24.
Whole number of Electors, 288.
ELECTORAL VOTE.—For President, Andrew Jackson, 219; Henry Clay, 49; John Floyd, 11: William Wirt, 7.
For Vice-President, Martin Van Buren, 189; John Sargent, 49; William Wilkins, 30; Henry Lee, 11: Amos Ellmaker, 7.
POPULAR VOTE.—For President, Jackson, 687,502; Clay, 550,189; Wirt and Floyd combined, 33,108.
Mr. Jackson was therefore declared the President elect, and Martin Van Buren, the Vice-President.

THIRTEENTH TERM—1837 TO 1841.

Whole number of States, 26.
Whole number of Electors, 294.
ELECTORAL VOTE.—For President, Martin Van Buren, 170; William H. Harrison, 73; Hugh L. White, 26; Daniel Webster, 14: W. P. Mangum, 11.
For Vice-President, Richard M. Johnson, 147; Francis Granger, 77; John Tyler, 47; William Smith, 23.
POPULAR VOTE.—For President, Van Buren, 762,149; all others combined, 736,736.
Mr. Van Buren was therefore declared the President elect, and Mr. Johnson the Vice-President.

FOURTEENTH TERM—1841 TO 1845.

Whole number of States, 26.
Whole number of Electors, 294.
ELECTORAL VOTE.—For President, Wm. H. Harrison, 234; Martin Van Buren, 60.
For Vice-President, John Tyler, 234; R. M. Johnson, 48; L. W. Tazwell, 11; James K Polk, 1.
POPULAR VOTE.—Harrison, 1,274,783; Van Buren, 1,128,702 James G. Birney, 7,609.

Mr. Harrison was therefore declared the President elect, and Mr. Tyler, the Vice-President.

FIFTEENTH TERM—1845 TO 1849.

Whole number of States, 26.
Whole number of Electors, 275.
ELECTORAL VOTE.—For President, James K. Polk, 170; Henry Clay, 105.
For Vice-President, George M. Dallas, 170; Theodore Frelinghuysen; 105.
POPULAR VOTE. — For President, Polk, 1,335,834; Clay, 1,297,033; Frelinghuyson, 105.

Mr. Polk was therefore declared the President elect, and Mr. Dallas the Vice President.

SIXTEENTH TERM.—1849 to 1853.

Whole number of States, 30.
Whole number of Electors, 290.
ELECTORAL VOTE. — For President, Zachary Taylor, 163; Lewis Cass, 127.
For Vice President, Millard Fillmore, 163; William O. Butler, 127.
POPULAR VOTE.—Taylor, 1,362,031; Cass, 1,222,445; Van Buren, 291,455.

Mr. Taylor was therefore declared the President elect, and Mr. Fillmore the Vice-President.

SEVENTEENTH TERM.—1853 to 1857.

Whole number of States, 31.
Whole number of Electors, 296.
ELECTORAL VOTE.—For President, Franklin Pierce, 254; Winfield Scott, 42.
For Vice-President, William R. King, 254; William A. Graham, 42.
POPULAR VOTE.—For President, Pierce, 1,590,490; Scott, 1,378,589; John P. Hale, 157,296.
Mr. Pierce was therefore declared the President elect, and Mr. King the Vice-President.

EIGHTEENTH TERM.—1857 to 1861.

Whole number of States, 31.
Whole number of Electors, 296.
ELECTORAL VOTE.—For President, James Buchanan, 174; John C. Fremont, 109; Millard Fillmore, 8.
For Vice-President, John C. Breckenridge, 174; William L. Dayton, 109. Andrew J. Donalson, 8.
POPULAR VOTE.—Buchanan, 1,832,232; Freemont, 1,341,-514; Millard Fillmore, 874,907.
Mr. Buchanan was therefore elected President, and Mr. Breckenridge the Vice-President.

NINETEENTH TERM.—1861 to 1865.

Whole number of States, 33.
Whole number of Electors, 303.
ELECTORAL VOTE.—For President, Abraham Lincoln, 180, John C. Breckenridge, 72; John Bell, 39; Stephen A. Douglass, 12.
For Vice-President, Hannibal Hamlin, 180; Joseph Lane, 72. Edward Everett, 39; H. V. Johnson, 12.
POPULAR VOTE.—Lincoln, 1,857,610; Douglass, 1,365,976; Breckenridge, 847,953; Bell, 590,631.
Mr. Lincoln was therefore elected President, and Mr. Hamlin the Vice-President.

TWENTIETH TERM.—1865 to 1869.

The States in rebellion did not vote in this election.
Number of States participating in the election, 25.
Whole number of Electors who voted, 233.

ELECTORAL VOTE.—For President, Abraham Lincoln, 212; George B. McClellan, 21.

For Vice-President, Andrew Johnson, 212; George H. Pendleton, 21.

POPULAR VOTE. — For President, 2,223,035; McClellan, 1,811,754.—Total vote, 4,034,789.

Mr. Lincoln was therefore re-elected President, and Mr. Johnson elected the Vice-Pressdent.

TWENTY-FIRST TERM.—1869 to 1873.

Whole number of States which voted, 34.
Whole number of Electors which voted, 294.

ELECTORAL VOTE.—For President, Ulysses S. Grant, 214; Horatio Seymour, 80.

For Vice-President, Schuyler Colfax, 214; Blair, 80.

POPULAR VOTE.—For President, Grant, 3,021,020; Seymour, 2,716,475.—Total, 5,737,495.

Virginia, Mississippi, and Texas did not take part in the election. The Legislature of Florida chose the Electors.

Grant and Colfax were therefore elected.

PRESIDENTIAL ELECTION OF 1868.

Popular, and Electoral Vote by States.

States.	Popular Vote.		Electoral Vote.		Majority
	Grant.	Seymour.	Grant.	Seymour	
Alabama........	76,366	72,086	8		4,280
Arkansas.......	22,150	19,080	5		3,070
California.....	54,575	54,069	5		506
Connecticut....	50,996	47,951	6		3,045
Delaware.......	7,623	10,980		3	*3,357
†Florida........			3		
Georgia........	57,134	102,822		9	45,688
Illinois........	250,293	199,143	16		51,150
Indiana........	176,552	166,980	13		9,572
Iowa...........	120,399	74,040	8		46,359
Kansas.........	31,046	14,019	3		17,027
Kentucky.......	39,566	115,889		11	*76,323
Louisiana......	33,263	80,225		7	*46,962
Maine..........	70,426	42,396	7		28,030
Maryland.......	30,408	63,357		7	*31,919
Massachusetts..	136,477	59,408	12		77,069
Michigan.......	128,550	97,069	8		31,481
Minnesota......	43,512	28,072	4		15,440
Mississippi....	No Election.				
Missouri.......	85,671	59,788	11		25,883
Nebraska.......	9,729	5,439	3		4,290
Nevada.........	6,480	5,218	3		1,262
New Hampshire..	38,191	31,224	5		6,967
New Jersey.....	80,121	83,001		7	*2,880
New York.......	419,883	429,883		33	*10,000
North Carolina.	96,226	84,090	9		12,136
Ohio...........	280,128	238,700	21		41,428
Oregon.........	10,961	11,125		3	*164
Pennsylvania...	342,280	313,382	26		28,898
Rhode Island...	12,993	6,548	4		6,445
South Carolina.	62,301	45,237	6		17,064
Tennessee......	56,757	26,311	11		30,446
Texas..........	No Election.				
Vermont........	44,173	12,051	5		32,122
Virginia.......	No Election.				
West Virginia..	29,025	20,306	5		8,719
Wisconsin......	108,857	84,710	8		24,147
	3,013,172	2,703,599	214	80	309,585

* Democratic Majority.
† Electors chosen by the Legislature.

THE WHITE HOUSE.

THE
LIBERAL REPUBLICAN CONVENTION

HELD IN CINCINNATI, MAY 1st, 1872.

CANDIDATES AND PLATFORM,

BIOGRAPHICAL SKETCHES, &C.

LIBERAL REPUBLICAN CONVENTION.

On the 1st day of May, 1872, Exposition Hall in Cincinnati, was crowded with delegates and spectators from all parts of the Union, to participate in, and witness the proceedings of the Liberal Republican Convention then and there convened. Great interest and excitement have ever attended this class of National gathering. At 12 o'clock, Colonel Grosvenor having called the Convention to order, made a few remarks and then named Judge Stanley Matthews of Ohio, as temporary Chairman.

The following day, the Committee on permanent organization, reported for permanent President, Senator Carl Shurz; with one Vice-President, and a Secretary from each State and Territory, which report was adopted. The Committee on Rules reported as follows:

First. That the rules and regulations governing the House of Representatives of the United States, shall be the rules governing this body, provided that no delegates shall be entitled to speak more than once upon the same question, and shall be limited to five minutes, except the mover thereof, who, in closing debate, shall be entitled to five minutes more.

Second. The delegation from each State shall cast the entire vote of the State, and every delegate shall represent such a proportion of the entire vote, as he shall be of the delegation present and his vote shall be reported to the Convention by the Chairman of the delegation as cast by the delegate.

Third. In voting for candidates for President and Vice-President of the United States, a majority of all the votes shall be requisite to a choice.

Fourth. To facilitate the business of the Convention, the Yeas and Nays shall not be called, but a division of the Convention may be had by a call of the States.

On the 3d day of May, Mr. Horace White, from the Committee on Platform, reported an address and a series of resolutions. The report was adopted. The following is the Address and Platform.

THE ADDRESS.

The Administration now in power, has rendered itself guilty of wanton disregard of the laws of the land, and usurped powers not granted by the Constitution. It has acted as if the laws had binding force only for those who are governed, and not for those who govern. It has thus struck a blow at the fundamental principles of constitutional government and the liberty of the citizen. The President of the United States has openly used the powers and opportunities of his high office for the promotion of personal ends. He has kept notoriously corrupt and unworthy men in places of power and responsibility to the detriment of the public interest. He has used the public service of the Government as a machinery of partisan and personal influence, and interfered with tyrranical arrogance in the political affairs of States and municipalities. He has rewarded, with influential and lucrative offices, men who had acquired his favor by valuable presents; thus stimulating demoralization of our political life by his conspicuous example. He has shown himself deplorably unequal to the tasks imposed upon him by the necessities of the country, and culpably careless of the responsibilities of his high office. The partisans of the Administration, assuming to be the Republican party, and controlling its organization, have attempted to justify such wrongs and palliate such abuses, to the end of maintaining partisan ascendency. They have stood in the way of necessary investigations and indispensable reforms, pretending that no serious fault could be found with the present administration of public affairs; thus seeking to blind the eyes of the people. They have kept alive the passions and resentments of the late civil war, to use them for their own advantage.

They have resorted to arbitrary measures in direct conflict with the organic law instead of appealing to the better instincts and latent patriotism of the Southern people, by restoring to them those rights, the enjoyment of which, is indispensible for a successful administration of their local affairs, and would tend to move a patriotic and hopeful national feeling. They have degraded themselves, and the name of their party, once justly entitled to the confidence of the nation, by a base sycophancy to the dispenser of executive power and patronage unworthy of Republican freemen; they have sought to stifle the voice of just criticism, to stifle the moral sense of the people, and to subjugate public opinion by tyrannical party discipline. They are striving to maintain themselves in authority for selfish ends, by an unscrupulous use of the power which rightfully belongs to the people, and should be employed only in the service of the country. Believing that an organization thus led and controlled can no longer be of service to the best interests of the Republic, we have resolved to make an independent appeal to the sober judgment, conscience, and patriotism of the American people.

THE PLATFORM.

We, the Liberal Republicans of the United States, in National Convention assembled at Cincinnati, proclaim the following principles as essential to just government:

First. We recognize the equality of all men before the law, and hold that it is the duty of Government, in its dealings with the people, to mete out equal and exact justice to all, of whatever nativity, race, color, or persuasion, religious, or political.

Second. We pledge ourselves to maintain the Union of these States, emancipation and enfranchisement, and to oppose any reopening of the questions settled by the Thirteenth, Fourteenth and Fifteenth Amendments to the Constitution.

Third. We demand the immediate and absolute removal of all disabilities imposed on account of the Rebellion, which was finally subdued seven years ago, believing that universal amnesty will result in complete pacification in all sections of the country.

Fourth. Local self-government, with impartial suffrage, will guard the rights of all citizens more securely than any centralized power. The public welfare requires the supremacy of the civil over the military authority, and freedom of person under the protection of the habeas corpus. We demand for the individual the largest liberty consistent with public order; for the State, self-government, and for the nation, to return to the methods of peace and the constitutional limitations of power.

Fifth. The Civil Service of the Government has become a mere instrument of partisan tyranny and personal ambition, and an object of selfish greed. It is a scandal and reproach upon free institutions, and breeds a demoralization dangerous to the perpetuity of republican government. We therefore regard such thorough reforms of the Civil Service as one of the most pressing necessities of the hour; that honesty, capacity, and fidelity constitute the only valid claim to public employment; that the offices of the Government cease to be a matter of arbitrary favoritism and patronage, and that public station become again a post of honor. To this end it is imperatively required that no President shall be a candidate for re-election.

Sixth. We demand a system of Federal taxation, which shall not unnecessarily interfere with the industry of the people, and which shall provide the means necessary to pay the expenses of the Government economically administered, the pensions, the interest on the public debt, and a moderate reduction annually of the principal thereof; and, recognizing that there are in our midst, honest, but irreconcilable differences of opinion, with regard to the respective systems of Protection and Free Trade, we remit the discussion of the subject to the people in their Congress Districts, and to the decision of Congress thereon, wholly free of Executive interference or dictation.

Seventh. The public credit must be sacredly maintained, and we denounce repudiation in every form and guise.

Eighth. A speedy return to specie payment, is demanded alike by the highest considerations of commercial morality and honest government.

Ninth. We remember with gratitude the heroism and sacrifices of the soldiers and sailors of the Republic, and no act of ours shall ever detract from their justly-earned fame, or the full reward of their patriotism.

Tenth. We are opposed to all further grants of lands to railroads, or other corporations. The public domain should be held sacred to actual settlers.

Eleventh. We hold that it is the duty of the Government, in its intercourse with foreign nations, to cultivate the friendship of peace, by treating with all on fair and equal terms, regarding it alike dishonorable either to demand what is not right, or submit to what is wrong.

Twelfth. For the promotion and success of these vital principles, and the support of the candidates nominated by this Convention, we invite and cordially welcome the co-operation of all patriotic citizens, without regard to previous affiliations.

HORACE GREELEY

NOMINATED FOR THE PRESIDENCY.

The next order of business being the Nomination of Candidates for the Presidency, the Chair stated that it would be done without the formal presentation of Candidates. The roll of States was then called.

FIRST BALLOT.

Adams, . . . 205	Brown, ... 95
Greeley, . . . 147	Curtin, . . . 62
Trumbull, . . . 110	Chase, . . . 2 1-2
Davis, . . . 92 1-2	

Total Vote, 614. Necessary to a choice, 308.

SECOND BALLOT.

Adams, . . . 243	Davis, ... 81
Greeley, . . . 239	Brown, . . . 2
Trumbull, . . . 148	Chase, ... 1

Total Vote, 714. Necessary to a choice, 358.

THIRD BALLOT.

Adams, . . . 264	Davis, ... 44
Greeley, . . . 258	Brown, . . . 2
Trumbull, . . . 156	

Total Vote, 714. Necessary to a choice, 358.

FOURTH BALLOT.

Adams, . . . 279	Davis, ... 51
Greeley, . . . 251	Brown, . . . 2
Trumbull, . . . 141	

Total Vote, 724. Necessary to a choice, 363.

FIFTH BALLOT.

Adams, . . . 309	Davis, . . . 30
Greeley, . . . 258	Chase, . . . 24
Trumbull, . . . 91	Brown, ... 2

Total Vote, 714. Necessary to a choice, 358.

SIXTH AND LAST BALLOT.

It was ordered amid a scene of great confusion. After the roll-call of States, it stood,

Greeley,	. . . 332	Chase,	. . .	32
Adams,	. . 324	Davis,	. . .	6
Trumbull,	. . 19	Palmer,	. . .	1

Before the vote was announced, Minnesota changed 9 from Trumbull to Greeley, and Pennsylvania changed 50 for Greeley, and 6 for Davis. Other changes were made, amid great noise and confusion.

The chair finally announced the result as follows:

Whole Vote,	. . 714	Greeley,	. . .	482
Necessary to a choice,	358	Adams,	. . .	187

Mr. Greeley was therefore the choice of the Convention.

B. GRATZ BROWN

NOMINATED FOR THE VICE-PRESIDENCY.

The Convention then proceeded to the Nomination of a Vice-President. It was announced that Mr. Trumbull would not except under any circumstances, and Cassius M. Clay declined to be a candidate.

Two ballots were taken. On the first, Mr. Brown received 237 votes. On the second ballot he received 435 votes, out of 696, the whole number cast, and was therefore the choice of the Convention for this office.

OFFICIAL NOTICE TO MR. GREELEY.

CINCINNATTI, Ohio, May 3, 1872.

Dear Sir:—The National Convention of the Liberal Republicans of the United States have instructed the undersigned, President, Vice-President, and Secretaries of the Convention, to inform you that you have been nominated as the candidate of the Liberal Republicans for the Presidency of the United States. We also submit to you the Address and Resolutions unanimously adopted by the Convention.

Be pleased to signify to us your acceptance of the platform and the nomination, and believe us very truly yours,

C. SCHURZ, *President.*
GEO. W. JULIAN *Vice-President.*

Wm. E. McLean,
John G. Davidson,
J. H. Rhodes,
F. W. Wright,
} *Secretaries.*

Hon. Horace Greeley, *New York City.*

MR. GREELEY'S REPLY.

New York, May 20, 1872.

Gentlemen:—I have chosen not to acknowledge your letter of the 3d inst, until I could learn how the work of your Convention was received in all parts of our great country, and judge whether that work was approved and ratified by the mass of our fellow-citizens. Their response has from day to day reached me through telegrams, letters, and the comments of journalists independent of official patronage, and indifferent to the smiles or frowns of power. The number and character of these unconstrained, unpurchased, unsolicited utterances satisfy me that the movement which found expression at Cincinnati has received stamp of public approval, and been hailed by a majority of our countrymen as the harbinger of a better day for the Republic.

I do not misinterpret this approval as especially complimentary to myself, nor even to the chivalrous and justly esteemed gentlemen with whose name I thank your Convention for associating mine. I receive and welcome it as a spontaneous and deserved tribute to that admirable Platform of principles, wherein your Convention so tersely, so lucidly, so forcibly, set forth the convictions which impelled, and the purposes which guided its course—a Platform which, casting behind it the wreck and rubbish of worn-out contentions and by-gone feuds, embodies in fit and few words the needs and aspirations of To-Day. Though thousands stand ready to condemn your every act, hardly a syllable of criticism or cavil has been aimed at your Platform, of which the substance may be fairly epitomized as follows:

I. All the political rights and franchises which have been acquired through our late bloody convulsion must and shall be guaranteed, maintained, enjoyed, respected, evermore.

II. All the political rights and franchises which have been lost through that convulsion, should and must be promptly restored and reestablished, so that there shall be henceforth no proscribed class and no disfranchised caste within the limits of our Union, whose long estranged people shall reunite and fraternize upon the broad basis of Universal Amnesty with Impartial Suffrage.

III. That, subject to our solemn constitutional obligation to maintain the equal rights of all citizens, our policy should aim at local self-government, and not at centralization; that the civil authority should be supreme over the military; that the writ of habeas corpus should be jealously upheld as the safeguard of personal freedom; that the individual citizen should enjoy the largest liberty consistent with public order; and that there shall be no Federal subversion of the internal polity of the several States and municipalities, but that each shall be left free to enforce the rights and promote the well-being of its inhabitants, by such means as the judgment of its own people shall prescribe.

IV. There shall be a real and not merely a simulated Reform in the Civil Service of the Republic; to which end it is indispensable that the chief dispenser of its vast official patronage shall be shielded from the main temptation to use his power selfishly by a rule inexorably forbidding and precluding his re-election.

V. That the raising of Revenue, whether by tariff or otherwise, shall be recognized and treated as the People's immediate business, to be shaped and directed by them through their Representatives in Congress, whose action thereon the

President must neither overrule by his veto, attempt to dictate, nor presume to punish, by bestowing office only on those who agree with him, or withdrawing it from those who do not.

VI. That the Public Lands must be sacredly reserved for occupation and acquisition by cultivators, and not recklessly squandered on the projectors of Railroads for which our people have no present need, and the premature construction of which is annually plunging us into deeper and deeper abysses of foreign indebtedness.

VII. That the achievment of these grand purposes of universal beneficence is expected and sought at the hands of all who approve them, irrespective of past affiliations.

VIII. That the public faith must at all hazards be maintained, and the National credit preserved.

IX. That the patriotic devotedness and inestimable services of our fellow-citizens who, as soldiers or sailors, upheld the flag and maintained the unity of the Republic shall ever be gratefully remembered and honorably requited.

These propositions, so ably and forcibly presented in the Platform of your Convention, have already fixed the attention and commanded the assent of a large majority of our countrymen, who joyfully adopt them, as I do, as the basis of a true, beneficent National Reconstruction—of a New Departure from jealousies, strifes, and hates, which have no longer adequate motive or even plausible pretext, into an atmosphere of Peace, Fraternity, and Mutual Good Will. In vain do the drill-sergeants of decaying organizations flourish menacingly their truncheons and angrily insist that the files shall be closed and straightened; in vain do the whippers-in of parties once vital, because rooted in the vital needs of the hour, protest against straying and bolting, denounce men nowise their inferiors, as traitors and renegades, and threaten them with infamy and ruin. I am confident that the American People have already made your cause their own, fully resolved that their brave hearts and strong arms shall bear it on to triumph. In this faith, and with the distinct understanding that, if elected, I shall be the President, not of a party, but of the whole People, I accept your nomination in the confident trust that the masses of our countrymen, North and South, are eager to clasp hands across the bloody chasm which has too long divided them, forgetting that they have been enemies, in the joyful consciousness that they are and must henceforth remain brethren.

Yours, gratefully,

HORACE GREELEY.

To Hon. Carl Schurz, President;
   Hon. George W. Julian, Vice-President; and
   Messrs. William E. McLean, John G. Davidson, J. H. Rhodes, F. W. Wright, Secretaries of the National Convention of the Liberal Republicans of the United States.

HORACE GREELEY.

BIOGRAPHICAL SKETCH.

On the 17th of August, 1831, a tall, pale and very plainly dressed young man of twenty years, with ten dollars in his pocket, and all his worldly goods tied up in a cotton handkerchief, which was made fast to a hickory stick swung over his shoulder, was seen leaving a steamer at Whitehall, New

HORACE GREELEY.

York city. His course was up Broad St. to Wall, thence across to West street, searching as he went for some boarding place, at a price within his means. At length, at No. 168 West street, he found a grog-shop and boarding-house combined, kept by one Mr. Golrick, where he obtained board and lodging at the stipulated price of $2.50 per week.

The name of this young man was Horace Greeley, of Scotch-Irish lineage, and a descendant of one of the three brothers who emigrated to America, in 1640. His father's name was Zaccheus Greeley, a poor and hard-working farmer who married his mother, Mary Woodburn, when she was but nineteen years of age.

Horace was born on the 3rd of February, 1811, in an unpainted, one-story frame house, which was facing the old road extending from the Merrimac, to Amherst in New Hampshire. Although a delicate, sickly child, he accomplished a great deal of hard labor as he grew older, assisting his father on the farm, spending however, a few months in each year at the village school.

In 1820, his father, who had been running behind was indebted to a few creditors to the amount of $1,000 and not being able to pay, they levied on his farm and personal property which were appraised and set off to the creditors at a nominal sum. The family soon removed to Vermont into a small dwelling which his father had hired for $16 per annum, and their poverty compelled them to live in the most frugal manner, principally on rye bread and Indian meal.

Horace remained assisting his father until his fifteenth year. In April 1826, he became an apprentice in the office of the publishers of the "Northern Spectator," at East Poultney, Vermont, where he was kindly treated and where, having access to a public library, he spent his leisure hours in reading and mental improvement. After completing his trade, he visited his parents, who had removed into New York state, and then was engaged for several months in the office of the Erie Gazette, at Erie, Pa., at $15 per month.

After dividing his earnings with his parents, to whom he was much attached, he started for New York city, with $25 in his pocket, and arrived there with but $10 left, as stated in the opening of this sketch. He obtained partial employment after a few days, at small wages, and in the spring and summer of 1832, obtained employment on the "Spirit of the Times," a weekly sporting paper.

In 1833, he and a Mr. Story opened a small printing establishment, doing principally job work; subsequently, in 1834, he edited "The New Yorker," a large weekly paper, which was published by himself and Mr. Winchester. He continued editing and publishing this paper for about seven years. He was, however, unfortunate. Having been burned out in the great Ann Street fire in 1835, being but partially insured, and meeting with many losses, and not being able to collect the subscriptions to his paper, which had accumulated to about $10,000, he was obliged to discontinue his paper, which he did in September, 1841.

In 1838, Mr. Thurlow Weed and other leading Whigs, having decided to start a cheap weekly campaign paper, to be called "The Jeffersonian." Mr. Greeley was selected as its editor, and offered $1,000 per annum to edit it, which offer he accepted. He subsequently, after the nomination of Harrison, edited and published a campaign paper, called the "Log Cabin," which had an immense circulation. On the 10th of April, 1841, Mr. Greeley issued the first number of "The New York Tribune," as a Whig paper. It was started as a cheap *daily* journal, at the price of one cent per copy, and has since proved to have been a most profitable and successful adventure. His first issue was 5,000, most of which were given away. His current expenses the first week was $525, while his receipts amounted to only $92. The subscriptions, however, to the paper, rapidly increased, and soon reached a circulation of 10,000 copies. For many years it was carried on, and prospered under Greeley & McElrath, who had formed a co-partnership soon after it was started.

For many years, it has been the leading Republican paper of the Union, and its receipts, as well as expenses, have been enormous. In 1866, its receipts amounted to over nine hundred thousand dollars. Its present circulation is several hundred thousand.

Mr. Greeley is in every sense of the word, a "self-made" man. He has been a hard worker, able reasoner, and deep thinker, and much attached to the *isms* of the day. Honest in his views and purposes, he has fearlessly and boldly given his opinions to the world; many of which have been original and peculiar

In 1848, he was elected to Congress, to fill a vacancy, and served for about three months. He has since visited Europe, and is the author of several literary works, and many tracts and essays. He is an able and vigorous writer, and quite popular as a lecturer.

Mr. Greeley was married July 5th, 1836, and of six children, but two are now remaining. Most of his leisure time is spent upon his farm, at *Chappaqua*, in Westchester Co., New York. about nine miles above White Plains, and about thirty-five miles from the City Hall in New York City. The farm embraces about seventy-five acres, twenty-five of which are covered with forest trees, in which he takes especial pride.

After the crushing out of the rebellion, he became with several others bail for Jefferson Davis, for which act, he was warmly condemned by some, but he alleges that it was done merely as an act of justice and humanity.

On the 3rd of May, 1872, at the convention of the Liberal Republicans, he was nominated for the Presidency, as hereinbefore stated, and subsequently on the 10th day of July, he was nominated by the National Democratic Convention, at Baltimore, an account of which is hereinafter given.

B. GRATZ BROWN.

BIOGRAPHICAL SKETCH.

This gentleman was born in Lexington, Kentucky, on the 28th of May, 1826. He is the son of Judge Mason Brown, an eminent jurist and magistrate of that State. His grandfather was John Brown, of Rockbridge, Va., who was a representative in Congress from 1789, to 1793. He subsequently remov-

B. GRATZ BROWN.

ed to Kentucky, settled at Frankfort, and was one of her first Senators after she was admitted into the Union.

His grandfather on the maternal side, was Jesse Bledsoe, a a distinguished jurist of Kentucky, who was elected to represent that State in the Senate of the United States. He was also a Chief Justice of the Supreme Court of Kentucky, and a professor of Law in the University of Transylvania.

B. Gratz Brown has received a most liberal education, and having passed through Transylvania University, he entered Yale College, from which he graduated in 1847. He subsequently studied law, and settled at St. Louis, Missouri. In 1852, he was elected to the Legislature of that State, where he represented his District for six years. He edited the *Missouri Democrat*, from 1854, to 1859. He was a strong Anti-Slavery man in that section of the Country, and took a bold and fearless stand against the exactions of the Slave power.

In 1857, he was the Free Soil Candidate for Governor, and came very near being elected. He took strong ground against the rebellion, and in the attack and capture of Camp Jackson, in 1861, he commanded a regiment of militia, and exhibited great coolness and gallantry. In 1863, he was elected to the Senate of the United States, where he served for four years. He was subsequently nominated for Governor of his State, and by a coalition of Democrats and Republicans he was elected, having received a majority of over 40,000.

Since his election to that office, Missouri has greatly extended her internal improvements, and is rapidly developing her immense resources. He is bold and decisive in action, energetic and persevering in all his undertakings, consults the happiness and prosperity of the masses, and as a Governor, is very popular.

At the Liberal Republican Convention, he received 95 votes on the 1st ballot for the Presidency, but at once declined in favor of Greeley. He then received on the first ballot for the Vice-Presidency 237 votes, and on the second 495, and was therefore declared the nominee of the Convention for that office. At the Democratic Convention at Baltimore, he also received the nomination for the same office

THE NATIONAL REPUBLICAN CONVENTION,

HELD IN PHILADELPHIA, JUNE 5, 1872.

CANDIDATES PLATFORM, &C.

THE NATIONAL REPUBLICAN CONVENTION.

At 12 o'clock, at noon, on the 5th day of June last, the Convention was called to order in the Academy of Music, at Philadelphia, by Gov. Claflin, who reminded the delegates of the glorious history of the Republican party during the past twenty years and asserted that the promises of reform and progress made four years ago, had been faithfully performed.

He then introduced the Honorable Morton McMichael as temporary Chairman, who in his remarks, stated that the people had decided in advance respecting the nominee, and that they had only to put their will into proper shape, by formally nominating Ulysses S. Grant, and with the blessing of God, they would make that nomination without demur, without debate, and without dissent. At about 4 o'clock, the Committee on permanent organization, reported Judge Settle of North Carolina for permanent Chairman, and Postmaster Bingham of Philadelphia, for permanent Secretary.

On the 6th of June, at 10 o'clock, A. M. the Convention reassembled in the Academy of Music, which was densely packed. After some preliminary exercises, Mr. McMichael presented a series of resolutions from the Union League of America, and by vote of the Convention, they were read and ordered to be entered on the minutes and printed. The resolutions set forth the principles of the Republican party, and urged the importance of faithfully standing by, and upholding them, against all foes of opposition and treachery.

NOMINATION OF U. S. GRANT FOR PRESIDENT.

After a few speeches had been made, Mr. Cullum of Illinois, arose and said, " *On behalf of the great Republican party of Illinois, and of the Union; in the name of liberty, loyalty, justice, law, interest of economy, good government, peace and equality of all before the law; remembering with gratitude, the achievements as a soldier in the field, and statesmanship in the Presidency, I renominate Ulysses S. Grant for the Presidency."*

This was received with the wildest enthusiasm, hats and handkerchiefs were waved, the music playing "Hail to the Chief," during which the curtain in the rear of the stage descended, disclosing a painting of Grant on horseback.

FIRST AND ONLY BALLOT.

The roll was then called for the first ballot, and as each State was called, the chairman of its delegation in a few remarks, announced its unanimous vote for Grant, and the result was, that he was unanimously renominated as the candidate for the next Presidency, and it was so announced by the chairman.

Previous to the balloting for the candidate for the Vice-Presidency, Mr. Schofield of Pennsylvania, chairman of committee on resolutions, announced that General Hawley of Connecticut, secretary of the committee, would read the resolutions, which were as follows:

PLATFORM.

Adopted by the Republican National Convention held at Philadelphia June 5th and 6th., 1872.

The Republican party of the United States, assembled in National convention, in the city of Philadelphia, on the 5th and 6th of June, 1872, again declares its faith, appeals to its history, and announces its positions upon the questions before the Country.

First—During eleven years of supremacy, it has accepted with grand courage the solemn duties of the time. It suppressed a gigantic rebellion, emancipated 4,000,000 of slaves, decreed the equal citizenship of all, and established universal suffrage. Exhibiting unparalleled magnanimity, it criminally punished no man for political offenses, and warmly welcomed all who proved their loyalty, by obeying the laws and dealing justly with their neighbors. It has steadily decreased with a firm hand, the resultant disorders of a great war, and initiated a wise policy towards the Indians. The Pacific railroad, and similar vast enterprises have been generously aided and successfully conducted, the public lands freely given to actual settlers, immigration protected and encouraged, and a full acknowledgement of the naturalized citizen's rights secured from European powers. A uniform national currency has been provided, repudiation frowned down, the national credit sustained under the most extraordinary burdens, and new bonds negotiated at lower rates. The revenues have been carefully collected, and honestly applied. Despite the annual large reduction of rates of taxation, the public debt has been reduced, during General Grant's Presidency, at the rate of $100,000.000 a year. A great financial crisis has been avoided, and peace and plenty prevail throughout the land. Menacing foreign difficulties have been peacefully and honorably compromised, and the honor and power of the nation kept in high respect throughout the world. This glorious record of the past, is the party's best pledge for the future. We believe the people will not entrust the government to any party, or combination of men composed chiefly of those who have resisted every step of this beneficial progress.

Second—Complete liberty, and exact equality in the employment of all civil, political and public rights should be established and effectually maintained throughout the Union, by efficient, and appropriate State and Federal legislation. Neither the law nor its administration should admit of any discrimination in respect of citizens by reason of race, creed, color or previous condition of servitude.

Third—The recent amendments to the national constitution should be cordially sustained because they are right, not merely tolerated because they are law, and should be carried out according to their spirit, by appropriate legislation, the enforcement of which, can be safely trusted only to the party that secured those amendments.

Fourth—The national government should seek to maintain honorable peace with all nations, protecting its citizens everywhere, and sympathising with all peoples who strive for greater liberty.

Fifth—Any system of the civil service under which the subordinate positions of the government are considered rewards for mere party-zeal is fatally demoralizing, and we therefore favor a reform of the system by laws which shall abolish the evils of patronage, and make honesty, efficiency, and fidelity the essential qualifications for public position, without practically creating a life tenure of office.

Sixth—We are opposed to further grants of the public lands to corporations and monopolies, and demand that the national domain be set apart for free homes for the people.

Seventh—The annual revenue, after paying the current expenditures, the pensions, and the interest on the debt, should furnish a moderate balance for the reduction of the principal, and that revenue, except so much as may be derived from a tax on tobacco and liquors, should be raised by duties upon importations, the detail of which should be so adjusted as to aid in securing remunerative wages to labor, and promote the industries, growth and prosperity of the whole country.

Eighth— We hold in undying honor the soldiers and sailors whose valor saved the union. Their pensions are a sacred debt by the nation, and the wi lows and orphans of those who died for their country are entitled to the care of a generous and grateful people. We favor such additional legislation as will extend the bounty of the government to all our soldiers and sailors who were honorably discharged, and who, in the line of duty, became disabled, without regard to the length of service or the cause of such discharge.

Ninth—The doctrine of Great Britain and other European powers concerning allegiance—"once a subject, always a subject"—having at last, through the efforts of the republican party, been abandoned, and the American idea of the individual's right to transfer allegiance, having been accepted by European nations, it is the duty of our government to guard with jealous care the rights of adopted citizens against the assumption of unauthorized claims by their former governments, and we urge the continued and careful encouragement and protection of voluntary immigration.

Tenth—The franking privilege ought to be abolished and the way prepared for a speedy reduction in the rates of postage.

THE NATIONAL REPUBLICAN PLATFORM. 215

Eleventh—Among the questions which press for attention, is that which concerns the relations of capital and labor, and the republican party recognizes the duty of so shaping legislation as to secure full protection and the amplest field for capital, and for labor, the creator of capital, the largest opportunities and a just share of the mutual profits of these two great servants of civilization.

Twelfth—We hold that Congress and the President have only fulfilled an imperative duty in their measures for the suppression of violent and treasonable organizations in certain lately rebellious regions, and for the protection of the ballot-box, and therefore they are entitled to the thanks of the nation.

Thirteenth—We denounce repudiation of the public debt in any form or disguise as a national crime. We witness with pride the reduction of the principal of the debt, and of the rates of interest upon the balance, and confidently expect that our excellent national currency will be perfected by a speedy resumption of specie payments.

Fourteenth—The republican party is mindful of its obligations to the loyal women of America for their noble devotion to the cause of freedom. Their admission into wider fields of usefulness is viewed with satisfaction, and the honest demands of any class of citizens for additional rights, should be treated with respectful consideration.

Fifteenth—We heartily approve the action of congress in extending amnesty to those lately in rebellion, and rejoice in the growth of peace and fraternal feeling throughout the land.

Sixteenth—The republican party proposes to respect the rights reserved by the people to themselves as carefully as the powers delegated by them to the state and to the federal governments. It disapproves of the resort to unconstitutional laws for the purpose of removing evils by interference with rights not surrendered by the people to either the State or the National Government.

Seventeenth—It is the duty of the General Government to adopt such measures as will tend to encourage American commerce and shipbuilding.

Eighteenth—We believe that the modest patriotism, the

earnest purpose, the sound judgment, the practical wisdom, the incorruptible integrity and the illustrious services of Ulysses S. Grant have commended him to the heart of the American people, and with him at our head we start to-day upon a new march to victory.

It was moved by General Burnside that the Platform as a whole be adopted, which motion was carried.

HENRY WILSON

NOMINATED FOR VICE PRESIDENT.

Henry Wilson and Schuyler Colfax, were the two leading Candidates proposed for this office, and both had warm and enthusiastic friends and it was doubtful which would obtain the nomination; hence there was great excitement during the balloting, and loud cheers were called forth on one side or the other as it progressed.

FIRST AND ONLY BALLOT.

At the close of the roll call, the vote stood as follows:

Wilson,	364 1-2	Davis,	16
Colfax,	321 1-2	Hawley,	1
Maynard,	25	Noyes,	1
Lewis,	22		

Whole number of Votes, 751.

At this stage, and before the result was announced, Virginia changed 20 of her votes to Wilson, making him 384 1-2, which gave him the nomination. Several other changes were subsequently made, when Mr. Crane of Indiana moved that Wilson's nomination be made unanimous, which was agreed to amidst great cheering.

Before the Adjournment of the Convention, the following Dispatch was received from Mr. Colfax.

WASHINGTON, JUNE 6.

John Foster, Indiana:—Accept for yourself and the delegation my sincere gratitude for your gallant contest. I support your ticket cheerfully. Men are nothing—principles everything. Nothing must arrest a republican triumph until equality under the law, like liberty from which it springs, is universally acknowledged, and the citizenship of the humblest becomes a sure protection against outrage and wrong, as was the Roman citizenship of old. (Signed) SCHUYLER COLFAX.

Judge Settle, the President of the Convention, and several of the Vice-Presidents, subsequently officially informed President Grant and Senator Wilson of their nomination. The following is the President's letter of acceptance:—

EXECUTIVE MANSION,
WASHINGTON, June 10, 1872.

The Hon. Thomas Settle, President of the National Republican Convention, Paul Strobach, Elisha Baxter, C. L. Sargent, and other Vice-Presidents:—

Gentlemen:—Your letter of this date, advising me of the action of the convention held in Philadelphia, on the 5th and 6th of this month, and of my unanimous nomination for the presidency by it, is received. I accept the nomination, and through you return my heartfelt thanks to your constituents for this mark of their confidence and support. If elected in November, and protected by a kind Providence in health and strength to perform the duties of the high trust conferred, I promise the same zeal and devotion to the good of the whole people for the future of my official life as shown in the past. Past experience may guide me in avoiding mistakes inevitable with novices in all professions, in all occupations. When relieved from the responsibilities of my present trust by the election of a successor, whether it be at the end of this term or the next, I hope to leave to him as executive, a country at peace within its own borders, at peace with outside nations, with credit at home and abroad, and without embarrassing questions to threaten its future prosperity.

With the expression of a desire to see a speedy healing of all bitterness of feeling between sections, parties, or races of citizens, and the time when the title of citizen carries with it all the protection and privileges to the humblest that it does to the most exalted, I subscribe myself,

Very Respectfully,
Your obedient servant,
U. S. GRANT.

The following is Senator Wilson's letter of acceptance.

WASHINGTON, D. C., June 14, 1872.

To the Hon. Thomas Settle and others, President and Vice-Presidents of the National Republican Convention, etc.:—

Gentlemen:—Your note of the 10th inst., conveying to me the action of the convention in placing my name in nomination for the office of Vice President of the United States, is now before me. I need not give you the assurance of my grateful appreciation of the high honor conferred upon me by this action of the fifth national convention of the republican party. Sixteen years ago, in the same city, was held the first meeting of the men who, amid the darkness and doubts of that hour of slaveholding ascendency and aggression, had assembled in national convention, to confer with each other on the exigencies to which that fearful domination had brought their country. After a full conference, the highest point of resolve they could reach, the most they dared to recommend, was the avowed purpose to prohibit the existence of slavery in the territories. Last week, the same party met by its representatives from 37 States and 10 Territories, at the same great center of wealth, intelligence, and power, to review the past, take note of the present, and indicate its line of action for the future. As typical facts of the headlands of the nation's recent history, there sat on its platform, taking prominent and honorable part in its proceedings, and admitted on terms of perfect equality to the leading hotels of the city, not only the colored representatives of the race, which were ten years before in abject slavery, but one of the oldest and most prominent, and once despised abolitionists, to whom was accorded, as to no other, the warmest demonstrations of popular regard and esteem, an ovation, not to him alone, but to the cause he had so ably, and for so many years represented, and the men and women, living and dead, who toiled through the long years of obloquy and self-sacrifice, for the glorious fruition of that hour. ' It hardly needed the brilliant summary of its platform to set forth its illustrious achievements. The very presence of those men was alone significant of victories already achieved, the progress already made, and the great distance which the nation had traveled between 1856 and 1872. But grand as has been its record, the republican party rests not on its past alone. It looks to the future, and grapples with its problems of duty and of danger. It proposes, as objects of its immediate accomplishments, "complete victory and exact equality to all," enforcement of recent amendments to the national constitution, reform in civil service, national domain to be set apart for homes of the people, the adjustment of duties on imports, so as to secure remunerative wages to labor, the extension of bounties to all soldiers and sailors who, in the line of duty became disabled, continual and careful encouragement and protection of voluntary immigration, and guarding with zealous care, the rights of adopted citizens; the abolition of the franking privilege, and a speedy reduction of the rates of postage, the reduction of the national debt, and rates of interest, and the resumption of specie payment; the encouragement of American Commerce and ship-building, the suppression of violence, and the protection of the ballot box. It also placed on record the opinions and purposes of the party in favor of amnesty against all the forms of repudiation, and endorsed the humane and peaceful policy of the administration in regard to the Indians. But while clearly defending, and distinctly announcing the policy of the republican party, on these questions of practical legislation and administration, the convention did not ignore the great social problems, which are pressing their claims for solution, and which demand the most careful study and wise consideration. Foremost stands the labor question. Concerning the relations of capital and labor, the republican party accepts the duty of so shaping legislation, as to secure full protection, and the amplest field for capital and for labor, the creation of capital, the largest opportunities, and a just share of the mutual profits of these two great servants of civilization. To woman, too, and her new demands, it extends hands of grateful recognition, and proffers its most respectful inquiry. It recognizes her noble devotion to country and freedom, welcomes her admission to wider fields of usefulness, and commends her demands for additional rights, to the calm and careful consideration of the nation. To guard well what has been secured, to work out faithfully and wisely what is now in hand, and to consider the questions which are looming up to view but a very little way before us, the republican party is to-day, what it was in the gloomy years of slavery, rebellion, and reconstruction, a national necessity. It appeals, therefore, for support, to the patriotic, and liberty-loving, to the just and humane, to all who would dignify labor, to all who would educate, elevate, and lighten the burdens of the sons and daughters of toil. With its great record, the work still to be done, under the great soldier whose historic renown, and whose successful administration for the last three years, begat popular confidence, the republican party may confidently, in the language of the convention you represent, start on a new march to victory. Having accepted, thirty-six years ago, the distinguishing doctrines of the republican party of to-day, having, during the years of that period, for their advancement, subordinated all other issues, acting in, and co-operating with political organizations, with whose leading doctrines, I sometimes had neither sympathy nor belief, having labored incessantly for many years, to found and build up the republican party, and having during its existence, taken a humble part in its grand work, I gratefully accept the nomination thus tendered, and shall endeavor, if it shall be ratified by the people, faithfully to perform the duties it imposes.

Respectfully yours,
HENRY WILSON.

HENRY WILSON.

BIOGRAPHICAL SKETCH.

This gentleman was born at Farmington, New Hampshire, on the 12th day of February, 1812, of poor, but respectable parents. At an early age, he was apprenticed to a farmer, with whom he remained till he was twenty-one years of age. His early education was necessarily very much neglected. He attended school only at short, irregular periods, which did not

HENRY WILSON.

exceed twelve months during the whole time he was upon the farm. Being, however, very fond of reading, he spent all his leisure moments in the perusal of such books as he could obtain, and thereby acquired a pretty thorough knowledge of men and of history.

At the age of twenty-one, he went to Natick, Mass., where he learned the trade of shoe-making, and accumulated a little money. Being desirous of obtaining an education, he commenced to study, but the person to whom he loaned his money having failed, he was obliged to go back to his trade at Natick, but not disheartened, he improved every opportunity to improve his mind, and cultivate his talents, turning his attention more particularly to political subjects

In 1840, he made several public political speeches, and the same year, at the age of twenty-eight years, he was elected to the Massachusetts Legislature, and having served there for four years, was elected to the Senate of that State, and was the president of that body for two sessions. He became a warm and earnest supporter of anti-slavery principles and sentiments, and when in 1848, being a delegate to the Whig National Convention, that body rejected the anti-slavery resolutions, he withdrew from the Convention, and became prominent in the organization of the Free-Soil party.

In 1852, he was chosen president of the Free-Soil National Convention in Pittsburg, and chairman of the National Committee. In the same year he was run on the Free-Soil ticket as a candidate for Congress, but was defeated by a small majority. In 1855, he was elected a Senator to succeed Edward Everett in Congress, and was re-elected in 1859 for a long term. Soon after taking his seat, he made strenuous efforts for the repeal of the fugitive slave law, and the abolition of slavery in the District of Columbia.

Senator Wilson was once challenged by Brooks, for denouncing his attack on Sumner, as "murderous, brutal, and cowardly," but refused to fight, condemning duelling as a barbarous practice. Shortly after the outbreak of the war, he raised the Twenty-Second Regiment of Massachusetts Volunteers, of which he was the Colonel, and after joining the army of the Potomac, was made a member of General McClellan's staff, in which capacity he served until the meeting of Congress.

During the war, he held the position of chairman of the Committe of Military Affairs, and as such, on the 4th of July,

1861, gave notice that on the following day he should ask leave to introduce six bills, having for their object the suppression of the rebellion, which bills, subsequently elicited much debate. He is acknowledged to be an earnest, skillful debator, and maintains his opinion with much warmth and zeal.

Senator Wilson has published several works, which are both valuable and interesting. He is one of the self-made men of the country, a most consistent and reliable man, respected and esteemed by men of all parties.

After being selected as a candidate, a large number of his fellow-townsmen in Natick, assembled to congratulate him upon his nomination, and the following is the conclusion of his address:

Friends—I stand before you to-night, having been supported over and over again for public life by your generous confidence. I count you all friends here to-night, of whatever political opinions you may be. It may be that there are those around me and about me, who have thought unkind thoughts, or said unkind words. I have forgotten them, and have no memory here for them to-night. I thank God that there is not a man or woman in my country that I cannot meet and offer the hand of friendship to.

Thanking you for your kindness, for the many evidences of your affectionate regard which I have received, and those near and dear to me have received, I will close by simply saying that whatever shall be the result in the country in the coming canvass—if defeat comes, I shall endeavor to bear it as I ought to do; if victory comes, I will simply say, I shall strive in the future as I have in the past to serve my country with fidelity, with clean hands and a pure heart, and to be true to the interests of my fellow men, and always to side with the weakest and poorest portion of my countrymen who need sympathy.

THE DEMOCRATIC NATIONAL CONVENTION,

HELD AT BALTIMORE, JULY 9, 1872.

CANDIDATES, PLATFORM, &C.

THE DEMOCRATIC NATIONAL CONVENTION.

On the 9th day of July, 1872, Ford's Opera House at Baltimore, was crowded with delegates, and at 12 o'clock at noon, the Convention was called to order by the Hon. August Belmont, Chairman of the National Committee, who, after some lengthy remarks, proposed Thomas Jefferson Randolph, of Virginia, a venerable gentleman of eighty years of age, and a grandson of Thomas Jefferson, as temporary Chairman.

After some preliminary business had been disposed of, Committees appointed, and the rules of the last Democratic National Convention adopted for the government of the Convention, a recess was taken until 4 o'clock, P. M.

After the Convention had reassembled, the Committee on Organization reported, for permanent President, James R. Doolittle of Wisconsin, who was conducted to the chair by Gov. Hoffman of New York, and Senator Bayard of Delaware.

After taking the chair, Mr. Doolittle made a very lengthy and earnest speech to the Convention, which was concluded amid long and continued applause.

Soon after 10 o'clock, A. M. on the following day, the Convention reassembled, and after being called to order Mr. A. E. Burr of Connecticut reported the resolutions which constituted the *Platform*.

Mr. Burr explained that the resolutions were the Cincinnati Platform exactly. Nothing added—nothing excluded. The preamble alone differed, it commenced as follows:

"We, the Democratic Electors of the United States in National Convention assembled, present the following principles, already proclaimed at Cincinnati, as essential to a just Government." (Then follow the Resolutions.)*

After the reading of the resolutions, Mr. Burr moved the adoption of the report, and moved the previous question. This course was warmly opposed by Mr. Bayard, who "did not believe in taking cut and dried, the resolutions of another

*For Platform see page 196.

organization." The previous question was sustained by a vote of 525 against 182, and the Platform was adopted by a vote of 670 against 62.

GREELEY AND BROWN NOMINATED.

Mr. Snowhook of Illinois, presented the name of Horace Greeley as the Democratic Candidate for the Presidency. The roll of the States was then called, which resulted as follows:

FOR PRESIDENT.

Greeley, . . . 686	Groesbeck, . . .	2
Bayard, . . . 16	Blank, . . .	7
Jerry Black, . . 21		

Whole number of Votes, 732.

FOR VICE-PRESIDENT.

B. Gratz Brown, . 713	Blank, . . .	13
Stevenson, . . . 6		

Whole number of Votes, 732.

On motion, the nomination of Greeley and Brown was made unanimous. Amid music and great enthusiasm, a scene was lowered in the rear of the stage, presenting a view of the White House. Soon after the Convention adjourned.

THE RATIFICATION AND ACCEPTANCE.

On the 12th of July, a little after noon, the large parlor of the Fifth Avenue Hotel in the city of New York was crowded by a company of distinguished and representative men, senators and ex-senators, congressmen, editors and governors were there from all parts of the union. Every state of the republic was represented by one or more of its most distinguished men. They were the committee appointed by the Baltimore convention to apprize Horace Greeley and B. Gratz Brown of their nomination for president and vice-president. After a brief conversation the committee left the hotel by twos, arm in arm, and walked to the Lincoln Club in East Twenty-first street, where awaiting them were Horace Greeley, Whitelaw

Reid, Gen. Cochrane, and a few others. Mr. Greeley sat in the back parlor of the club house talking with a few friends when the committee arrived and expressed great surprise at their early appearance. He said he had not expected to receive the committee until late in the afternoon. Mr. Greeley was dressed in an alpaca coat, black pantaloons, white vest, spotless shirt, and well-blacked boots, while on the table to his right, rested the historical white hat. As the committee filed into the room, almost filling it, Mr. Greeley advanced to the little table in its center, and placing one hand on the table, awaited the pleasure of his visitors.

Augustus Schell, president of the national democratic executive committee, introduced Mr. Doolittle, chairman of the Baltimore convention, to Mr. Greeley. After cordial greetings were exchanged, Mr. Doolittle read from manuscript the following brief address :—

DOOLITTLE'S SPEECH,

Mr. Greeley, the national democratic convention recently held at Baltimore charged us with the pleasing duty of waiting upon you in person to notify you of its unanimous nomination of yourself as candidate for the presidency. We were informed it would be agreeable to you to meet us here at this time, and we have come in a body to place in your hands this official notification. The published proceedings of our convention show great unanimity, but those only who took part in them can realize the cordiality and enthusiasm with which it resolved to sustain the Liberal Republican movement, to co-operate with all patriotic citizens to support the principles declared at Cincinnati, and resolved also, as the best and surest mode of giving effect to those great principles, to nominate and elect the same candidate. We both witnessed and felt that cordiality and enthusiasm. Mr. Greeley, allow me to introduce to you the members of the committee.

When the ceremony of introduction was over, Mr. Greeley took his position in the center of the room, and spoke slowly and deliberately, as follows :—

GREELEY'S REPLY.

I should need time were I to attempt to reply fitly and fully to the important, and I need not say gratifying communication. It may be that I should reply in writing, but as I have lately addressed a letter, which has been pretty widely considered, to the Liberal Republican Convention, it may not be necessary. I can only say now, that I accept your nomination, accept it gratifyingly in the spirit in which it was offered I am at present in a position which, doubtless, many would regard as a proud one, but which is still an embarrassing one, because it involves the temporary, and I trust only temporary, annoyance of a misconstruction of my motives on the part of some valued and life-long friends. I am confident that time alone is necessary to vindicate my motives to all candid observers, and to convince all indeed of the disinterestedness and patriotism of the course I am pursuing, and intended to pursue long before I was assured of so much co-operation and sympathy. The time will come, and I trust in God the opportunity too, when the world will see that you are no less democrats because you have pursued the course you have, and that I am no less a republican because I accept your nomination. (Here Mr. Greeley's voice faltered with emotion. He recovered himself and continued.) I am not much in the habit of receiving nominations for the presidency, and I am consequently unable to reply as readily and fluently as others might. I can only say that I shall be happy to see all of you, or at least as many of you as can come, at my humble farmer home, where I shall be to-morrow, and where we shall be able to converse and confer more freely than here. If you will come, I shall be happy to make you welcome to the best the farm affords and so I simply wish you farewell.

MR GREELEY'S FORMAL ACCEPTANCE OF THE BALTIMORE NOMINATION.

NEW YORK, July 23.—The following is Mr. Greeley's acceptance of the Baltimore nomination:—

MR. GREELEY'S ACCEPTANCE.

NEW YORK, July 18, 1872.

Gentlemen—Upon mature deliberation it seems fit that I should give to your letter, of the 10th inst., some further and fuller response than the hasty, unpremeditated words in which I acknowledged and accepted your nomination at our meeting on the 12th. That your convention saw fit to accord its honor to one who had been prominently and pointedly opposed to your party in the earnest and sometimes angry controversies of the last forty years, is essentially noteworthy. That many of you originally preferred that the Liberal Republicans should present another candidate for president, and would more readily have united with us in the support of Adams, or Trumbull, Davis or Brown, is well known. I owe my adoption at Baltimore wholly to the fact that I had already been nominated at Cincinnati, and that the concentration of forces upon any new ticket had been proved impracticable. Gratified as I am at your concurrence in the Cincinnati nominations, certain as I am that you would not have thus concurred, had you not deemed me upright and capable, I find nothing in the circumstance calculated to inflame my vanity, or nourish self-conceit, but that your convention saw fit, in adopting the Cincinnati ticket, to reaffirm the Cincinnati platform, is to me a source of the profoundest satisfaction. That body was constrained to take this important step by no party necessity, real or supposed. It might have accepted the candidates of the Liberal Republicans upon grounds entirely its own, or it might have presented them as the first Whig National Convention did Harrison, without adopting any platform whatever. First, it chose to plant itself deliberately by a vote nearly unanimous upon the fullest and clearest enunciation of principles which are at once incontestably republican and emphatically democratic, gives trustworthy assurance that a new and more auspicious era is dawning upon our long distracted country. Some of the best years and best efforts of my life have been devoted to a struggle against chattel slavery, a struggle none the less earnest or arduous, because respect for constitutional obligations constrained me to act for the most part on the defensive in resistance to the diffusion, rather than in direct efforts for the extinction of human bondage. Throughout most of those years my vision was uncheered. My exertions were rarely animated by even so much as a hope that I should live to see my country peopled by freemen alone. The affirmance of the Cincinnati platform is a most conclusive proof that not merely is slavery abolished, but that its spirit is extinct, that despite the protest of a respectable but isolated few, there remains among us no party or formidable interests which regrets the overthrow or desires the re-establishment of human bondage, whether in letter or spirit. I am thereby justified in my hope and trust, that the first century of American independence will not close, before the grand elemental truths on which its rightfulness was based by Jefferson and the Continental Congress of '76, will no longer be regarded as glittering generalities, but will have become the universally accepted and honored foundation of our political fabric. I demand the prompt application of those principles to our existing condition. Having done what I could for the complete emancipation of the blacks, I now insist on the full enfranchisement of all my white countrymen. Let none say the ban has just been removed from all but a few hundred elderly gentlemen, to whom eligibility to office can be of little consequence. My view contemplates, not the hundreds proscribed, but the millions who are denied the right to be ruled and represented by the men of their unfettered choice. Proscription were absurd if these did not wish to elect the very men whom they are forbidden to choose. I have a profound regard for the people of New England, wherein I was born, in whose common schools I was taught. I rank no other people above them in intelligence, capacity, and moral worth, but where they do many things well, and some admirably, there is one thing which I am sure they cannot wisely or safely undertake, that is, the selection of states remote unlike their own, of the persons by whom those states shall be represented in congress. If they could do this to good purpose, then republican institutions were unfit, and aristocracy the only true political system. Yet what have we recently witnessed? Zebulon B. Vance, the unquestioned choice of a large majority of the present legislature of North Carolina, a majority backed by a majority of the people who voted at its election, refused the seat in the Federal Senate to which he was fairly chosen, and the legislature was thus constrained to choose another in his stead, or leave the State unrepresented for years. The votes of New England thus deprived North Carolina of the senator of her choice, and compelled her to send another in his stead: —another, who in our late contest was like Vance, a rebel, and a fighting rebel, but who had not served in congress before the war, as Vance had, though the latter remained faithful to the union until after the close of his term. I protest against the disfranchisement of a State, presumptively of a number of

States, on grounds so narrow and technical as this. The fact that the same Senate which refused Vance his seat proceeded to remove his disabilities after that seat had been filled by another, only serves to place in stronger light the indignity to North Carolina, and the arbitrary conspicuous tyranny which dictated it. I thank you, gentlemen, that my name is to be conspicuously associated with yours in a determined effort to render amnesty complete and universal, in spirit as well as in letter. Even defeat in such a cause would leave no sting, while triumph would rank with those victories which no blood reddens, and which evoke no tears but those of joy.

Gentlemen, your platform which is also mine, assures me that democracy is not henceforth to stand for one thing, and republicanism for another, but that those terms are to mean in politics, as they always have meant in the dictionary, substantially one and the same thing, namely, equal rights regardless of creed, or clime, or color. I hail this as a genuine new departure from outworn feuds and meaningless contentions in the direction of progress and reform. Whether I shall be found worthy to bear the standard of the great liberal movement which the great American people have inaugurated is to be determined, not by words, but deeds. With me, if I steadily advance, over me, if I falter, its grand array moves on to achieve for our country her glorious beneficent destiny. I remain, gentlemen, yours,

HORACE GREELEY.

NATIONAL PROSPERITY.

Less than ninety years ago, we were composed of thirteen feeble colonies with three millions of inhabitants, occupying the original narrow strip of land on the Atlantic coast, which has since expanded into a mighty empire, extending westward to the very shores of the Pacific, and northward to the Northern Lakes, including the Arctic regions of Alaska. Forty-five years ago, a railroad was unknown, while there are now over 53,000 miles of these roads, constructed at a cost of twenty-five hundred millions of dollars, besides 80,000 miles more projected and in progress, connecting all parts of our land and linking together the two great oceans.

We have now more than 150,000 miles of telegraph wires, enabling the people in these widely separated States to exchange intelligence more rapidly, than could have been done forty years ago between the towns of a single County. The stage coach, the canal packet, couriers on horseback and other such modes of conveyance are becoming as much things of the past, as the tinder-box, pounding-barrels, and saddle-bags of olden times.

The inventive talents and genius of our people have wonderfully developed the productive power, and agricultural resources of the Country. In 1836, Congress presumed that a commissioner and one clerk were sufficient to do all the work of the Patent Office. Over 60 examiners are now employed, and a force of 300 employees are necessary to do the work of the Office. About 20,000 patents are issued annually.

How vast and productive are the sources of wealth and prosperity in our mines of gold, silver, copper, petroleum, in our fisheries and fur trade, and in our forests of pine! what stupendous monuments of Yankee ingenuity and Yankee enterprise do we see around us.

If we still continue to exercise those three political virtues, industry, frugality and economy, and still continue an united people, in all human probability the year 1900 will find us the most powerful nation that ever existed, with a population of one hundred millions.

www.ingramcontent.com/pod-product-compliance
Lightning Source LLC
Chambersburg PA
CBHW022006220426
43663CB00007B/988